SR

Moral Exhortation,
A Greco-Roman Sourcebook

Library of Early Christianity

Wayne A. Meeks, General Editor

Moral Exhortation,
A Greco-Roman Sourcebook

Abraham J. Malherbe

The Westminster Press
Philadelphia

Book design by Gene Harris

First edition

Published by The Westminster Press®
Philadelphia, Pennsylvania

PRINTED IN THE UNITED STATES OF AMERICA

9 8 7 6 5 4 3 2 1

Library of Congress Cataloging-in-Publication Data

Moral exhortation.

(Library of early Christianity ; v. 4)
Bibliography: p.
Includes indexes.
1. Ethics. 2. Conduct of life. 3. Philosophy,
Ancient. I. Malherbe, Abraham J. II. Series: Library
of early Christianity ; 4.
BJ211.M67 1986   170′.938   86-5499
ISBN 0-664-21908-X

Contents

Foreword by Wayne A. Meeks   7

Acknowledgments   9

Introduction   11

Sources   17

1. The Social Settings of Moral Instruction   23

2. The Aims and Character of the Moral Teacher   30
    The Goal of Philosophy   30
    The Philosopher and His Task   34
      Begins with Himself   34
      Conformity of Speech to Life   38
    The Human Condition   40

3. Methods of Instruction and Moral Nurture   48
    Instruction of Groups and Individuals   48
    Adaptation to Circumstances   50
    The Response Sought   55
    Attitudes and Practices Taught   59

4. Means of Instruction   68
    Speeches   68
    Letters   79
    Epitomes   85

Compilations   105
Summaries of a Philosopher's Teaching   105
Advice on a Particular Subject   107
Gnomes   109
Chreiai   111
Poetry   115
The Use of Philosophic Compilations   117

5. Styles of Exhortation   121
Protrepsis   122
Paraenesis   124
Diatribe   129

6. Literary and Rhetorical Conventions   135
Personal Examples   135
Lists of Virtues and Vices   138
Lists of Hardships   141

7. Conventional Subjects   144
On the State   145
On Civil Concord   147
On Retirement   148
On Civic Responsibility   149
On the Professions   150
On Sexual Conduct   152
On Covetousness   154
On Anger   157
On Slavery and Freedom   158
On the Armor of the Sage   159

Bibliography   163

Index of Names   165

Index of Subjects   168

Index of New Testament References   175

Index of Apostolic Fathers References   178

Foreword

This series of books is an exercise in taking down fences. For many years the study of ancient Christianity, and especially of the New Testament, has suffered from isolation, but happily that situation is changing. For a variety of reasons, we have begun to see a convergence of interests and, in some instances, real collaboration by scholars across several academic boundaries: between Roman historians and historians of Christianity, between New Testament scholars and church historians, between historians of Judaism and of Christianity, between historical and literary scholars.

The Library of Early Christianity harvests the fruit of such collaboration in several areas in which fresh approaches have changed the prevailing view of what the early Christians were like. Much of what is presented here has not been brought together in this fashion before. In order to make this information as accessible as possible, we have not burdened the books with the sort of argument and documentation that is necessary in scholarly monographs, in which such new work is ordinarily presented. On the other hand, the authors do not condescend to their readers. Students in colleges and seminaries and at more advanced levels will find in these books an opportunity to participate in a conversation at the growing edge of current scholarship.

The common perspective of the series is that of social history. Both words of the phrase are equally important. The objects of study are the living Christian communities of the early centuries in their whole environment: not just their ideas, not only their leaders and heroes. And the aim is to understand those communities as they believed, thought, and acted then and there—not to "explain" them by some supposedly universal laws of social behavior.

What has Athens to do with Jerusalem? is an old question, and since Tertullian posed it, derisively, it has been answered in many different ways. Just now the debate has become especially lively, in this form: What did the moral teachings of the early Christian writers owe to the pagan philosophers and orators of their time, and in what particulars were the Christian teachings distinctive, either in style or in content? One of the sagest leaders in this discussion, and one of the most knowledgeable about the philosophical and rhetorical schools in the early Roman empire, is Abraham J. Malherbe. In this volume he has brought together primary materials with concise but penetrating introductions. With these in hand, a reader can begin an immediate engagement with the ancient ways of thinking and talking about ethics and can compare them directly with the New Testament and other early Christian literature.

WAYNE A. MEEKS
General Editor

Acknowledgments

I am grateful for permission to reprint selections from the following works:

Cicero, *De Officiis*, trans. Walter Miller (Cambridge, Mass.: Harvard University Press, 1913). Reprinted by permission of the publishers and The Loeb Classical Library.

Pseudo-Crates, *Epistles*, trans. Ronald F. Hock, in *The Cynic Epistles*, ed. Abraham J. Malherbe (Missoula, Mont.: Scholars Press, 1977). Reprinted by permission of the publisher.

Pseudo-Demetrius, *Epistolary Types*, trans. Abraham J. Malherbe, *Ohio Journal of Religious Studies* 5 (1977). Reprinted by permission of the publisher.

Pseudo-Diogenes, *Epistles*, trans. Benjamin Fiore, S.J., in *The Cynic Epistles*, ed. Abraham J. Malherbe (Missoula, Mont.: Scholars Press, 1977). Reprinted by permission of the publisher.

Dio Chrysostom, *Discourses*, Vols. 1, 2, 3, 4, and 5, trans. J. W. Cohoon and H. Lamar Crosby (Cambridge, Mass.: Harvard University Press, 1932, 1939, 1940, 1946, 1951). Reprinted by permission of the publishers and The Loeb Classical Library.

Diogenes Laertius, *Lives of Eminent Philosophers*, Vols. 1 and 2, trans. R. D. Hicks (Cambridge, Mass.: Harvard University Press, 1938, 1925). Reprinted by permission of the publishers and The Loeb Classical Library.

Epictetus, *Discourses*, Vols. 1 and 2, trans. W. A. Oldfather (Cambridge, Mass.: Harvard University Press, 1925, 1928). Reprinted by permission of the publishers and The Loeb Classical Library.

Horace, *Satires, Epistles, and Ars poetica*, trans. H. R. Fairclough (Cambridge, Mass.: Harvard University Press, 1926). Reprinted by permission of the publishers and The Loeb Classical Library.

Isocrates, Vol. 1, *To Demonicus,* trans. George Norlin (Cambridge, Mass.: Harvard University Press, 1928). Reprinted by permission of the publishers and The Loeb Classical Library.

Julian, *Orations,* Vol. 2, trans. Wilmer Cave Wright (Cambridge, Mass.: Harvard University Press, 1913). Reprinted by permission of the publishers and The Loeb Classical Library.

Lucian, Vols. 1, 2, and 3, trans. A. M. Harmon (Cambridge, Mass.: Harvard University Press, 1913, 1915, 1921). Reprinted by permission of the publishers and The Loeb Classical Library.

Maximus of Tyre, *Orations,* trans. in Arthur O. Lovejoy and George Boas, *Primitivism and Related Ideas in Antiquity* (Baltimore: Johns Hopkins University Press, 1935). Reprinted by permission of the publisher.

Musonius Rufus, from Cora E. Lutz, *Musonius Rufus: "The Roman Socrates,"* Yale Classical Studies, Vol. 10 (1947). Reprinted by permission of the publisher.

Pliny, *Letters,* Vol. 2, trans. William Melmoth (Cambridge, Mass.: Harvard University Press, 1915). Reprinted by permission of The Loeb Classical Library and the publisher.

Plutarch, *Parallel Lives,* Vol. 9, trans. Bernadotte Perrin (Cambridge, Mass.: Harvard University Press, 1920). Reprinted by permission of the publishers and The Loeb Classical Library.

Plutarch, *Moralia,* Vols. 1, 2, and 15, trans. Frank C. Babbitt and F. H. Sandbach (Cambridge, Mass.: Harvard University Press, 1927, 1928, 1969). Reprinted by permission of the publishers and The Loeb Classical Library.

Seneca, *Epistulae Morales,* Vols. 1, 2, and 3, trans. Richard M. Gummere (Cambridge, Mass.: Harvard University Press, 1917, 1920, 1925). Reprinted by permission of the publishers and The Loeb Classical Library.

Seneca, *Moral Essays,* Vol. 1, trans. John W. Basore (Cambridge, Mass.: Harvard University Press, 1928). Reprinted by permission of the publishers and The Loeb Classical Library.

Sextus Empiricus, Vol. 1, *Outlines of Pyrrhonism,* trans. R. G. Bury (Cambridge, Mass.: Harvard University Press, 1933). Reprinted by permission of the publishers and The Loeb Classical Library.

Introduction

The moral teaching of early Christians in many ways resembled that of their pagan neighbors. Celsus, the great opponent of Christianity in the second century, charged that Christian teaching was commonplace and derived from the pagan philosophers (Origen, *Against Celsus* 1.4). Most educated Christians from the second century on acknowledged the similarities, and some made overt use of the teachings and literary works of the pagan moralists. Modern scholars have shown that already the earliest Christian writers, represented in this book by the New Testament and the apostolic fathers, were considerably indebted to their pagan predecessors and contemporaries for how and what they taught. The passages included here represent some typical features and illustrate Christianity's indebtedness to the Greco-Roman moral tradition.

It is not always clear how elements from this tradition found their way into Christianity. Sometimes Christian writers appropriated material, consciously or unconsciously, directly from the pagan supply at their disposal. But Jews had already done the same, and sometimes material from the moral tradition came to Christians in a form given it by this Jewish adaptation of the tradition. The material collected in this book therefore represents one moral tradition which contributed to Judaism as well as to Christianity.

That Celsus compared Christians' ethics with the philosophers' was natural, for philosophy was generally regarded as the preeminent guide to the moral life. The relationship between the traditional Greek gods and morality appears to have been ambiguous, for while the gods were thought to punish wrongs, they themselves are represented as acting immorally. They were criticized in the fifth century B.C., particularly in Greek tragedy and comedy, on moral grounds. In a general way such criticism lessened the influence of religion on morality. During the Hellenistic period, it was the conviction that reason was the basis for the moral life, and the philosophers increasingly turned their attention to ethics. Convinced that right conduct depends on correct knowledge, they tended to fit ethics into a comprehensive system. During this period, this was accomplished by teaching ethics as one of three divisions of philosophy, the other two being logic and physics.

The major philosophical schools or sects during the Hellenistic and Roman periods were the Platonists, Stoics, Cynics, and Epicureans. (See Wayne A. Meeks, *The Moral World of the First Christians* [Philadelphia: Westminster Press, 1986], ch. 2.) They retained their individual differences in the ways they defined precisely the goal of human life and in their positions on some particular matters, but in general their teachings tended to blend. A number of factors contributed to this blending. Philosophy came to be taught with the aid of handbooks that treated ethics as a distinct division that could be separated from the rest of the system, which thus became relativized. The attacks by the Skeptics on the dogmatic parts of the system further contributed to this separation and to a stress on what appeared to be self-evidently right, irrespective of the philosophical system that might originally have provided a logical framework for it. It was also the practice to study with philosophers of different schools, so a person would be likely to come away with an eclectic moral system, derived from various teachers. In the Roman empire, Stoicism predominated in this philosophical blend.

It is easy to overstress this so-called "philosophical Koine," for there were differences between the schools and sometimes between members of the same school. For example, Plutarch, who was a Platonist, wrote numerous tractates against the Epicureans and the Stoics, even though he was indebted to Stoicism for some of his own teaching. And Cynics disagreed among themselves on what the moral condition of people in general was and on the proper way to correct it. Philosophers so often attacked each other that the abuse they heaped on each other became stereotyped. Epicureans were accused of atheism, hedonism, and hatred of humanity, Stoics of greed and contentiousness, Peripatetics of quarrelsomeness and greed, Platonists of arrogance and ambition, Pythagoreans of reclusiveness and abstraction, and Cynics of being a low-class mob who degraded philosophy by their ignorance, effrontery, and vulgarity.

Nevertheless, despite this antipathy to each other and such differences between their systems as the Skeptics, for instance, could point to, philosophers of different persuasion had much in common. They tended to share the conviction that the moral life was lived according to nature, even though they differed in details on what they meant by nature, and they related virtue to knowledge and vice to ignorance. Happiness, they thought, was to be attained through knowledge, by which human shortcomings were to be overcome and personal fulfillment reached. This attainment of virtue was equivalent to fulfilling one's potential as a human being through the disciplined, rational life. They also tended to be strongly individualistic, stressing self-sufficiency and drawing attention to the figure of the ideal wise man who had attained the good life and thus possessed virtue, a human achievement of which he could be justly proud. In addition to sharing such views, they also used many of the same methods in teaching people and guiding them in their moral growth.

Greek philosophy was introduced to Rome in a systematic manner by Cicero in the first century B.C., and further spread after the fall of the republic. A suspicion that philosophy was too theoretical, however, lingered among some more practically minded Romans, and some emperors during the first century of the empire had cause to think that philosophy, Stoicism in particular, could be responsible for opposition to the state. But philosophical ethics became popularized and penetrated many levels of society. Evidence for this is found in many sources, such as letters, which, except for ethics, reflect no other interest in philosophy, in descriptions of popular opinions and mores by satirists, and in speeches delivered to the masses which assume familiarity, if only on a superficial level, with philosophic teaching.

The settings in which philosophy was taught contributed to this popularization of philosophical ethics. Philosophers were invited to deliver discourses on moral topics in the salons of the wealthy; some of them spoke, when invited, to gatherings in the forum or such places as the public baths; and others were attached to the homes of persons of means or joined the retinues of governmental officials. Other philosophers taught in their own homes or in rented quarters, while still others, like the Epicureans, withdrew from society to form philosophic communities. Some Stoics, but especially Cynics, preached in the marketplaces and on street corners, where they urged all who passed by to listen to them as they spoke of virtue. In addition, beginning around the age of fifteen, schoolboys were given elementary instruction in philosophy in the hope that it would guide them throughout their lives. Philosophers such as Musonius Rufus and Epictetus also conducted schools in which they provided more advanced instruction for young men who were preparing for public life.

Modern scholarship has shown that the writers of the New Testament and the apostolic fathers derived much from these philosophers. These Christian writers on occasion describe themselves and other teachers in language derived from the philosophers. They also owe to the philosophers some of the forms in which they cast their instruction, the styles they adopted to achieve particular ends, and even some of the subjects they chose to discuss. The selections from the philosophers included in this book almost all come from the first and second centuries A.D. and are intended to cast light on the relationship between early Christian moral exhortation and its Greco-Roman counterpart. Such an attempt is fraught with dangers of which readers of this book should be aware.

As the ancient handbooks and summaries of philosophic teachings led to harmonization, and even homogenization, of the different authors and their views, so may the present compilation. This danger, which is inherent in all compilations, is made greater by the fact that the material is likely to be viewed through a Christian lens, which may make it appear to have greater unity than it in fact has. Some efforts have been made to minimize this risk. The book has been organized in a manner designed to protect the integrity of the pagan material, the excerpts have been kept as long as possible so as not to leave the reader with snippets taken out of any meaningful context, and the wide range of texts included, from Platonists, Peripatetics, Cynics, Stoics, Epicureans, Pythagoreans, and a Skeptic, is intended not only to demonstrate what they share but to invite comparison of different authors and philosophic traditions. The cross references, given in boldface type, and the indexes should make it possible at least to begin such a comparison, but there is no substitute for reading in the moral literature itself, and readers will do well to heed Seneca's caution on the use of compilations (**47**).

As the pagan material does not represent a seamless whole, so does not the Christian material to which reference is made in the introductions to the individual selections. The diversity in ethical outlook within the Christian material is well known; here it needs to be added that Christian attitudes toward pagan morality were equally complex. On the one hand, they regarded their pre-Christian pagan lives as a morass from which they were thankful to have been delivered (cf. 1 Cor. 6:9–11; Eph. 2:1–3; Titus 3:3; 1 Peter 1:18) and to which they were now superior (cf. 1 Cor. 5:1; 1 Thess. 4:5). On the other hand, by urging that Christian behavior would bring honor to God and respect to the faith and the faithful, they presupposed an agreement with the standards of their society (cf. 1 Cor. 10:32; Col. 4:5; 1 Thess. 4:12; 1 Tim. 3:7; 6:1; Titus 2:5, 8, 10; 1 Peter 2:12, 15; 3:1, 16; 1 Clem. 1.1; 47.7; Ignatius, *Trall.* 8.2).

Furthermore, some Christian writings—for example, the pastoral epistles—are more closely related to the Greco-Roman moral tradition than are others.

This all having been said, it is yet possible to venture some generalizations on pagan philosophical and Christian ethics. From the first century B.C., philosophy became increasingly open to religion. The way in which Stoics of the period speak of the divine frequently suits a conception of a personal god better than it does Stoic pantheism. And the Neopythagorean motivation for ethics is religious in the sense that it aims at purifying the person of the material body so that after death he might return to the nonmaterial world. Yet the philosophers retained their stress on reason and reliance on self in striving for virtue. Christians, on the other hand, stressed reliance on God, Christ, and the Holy Spirit, and considered the moral life a corollary to their knowledge of God and the divine will. They therefore very seldom spoke of virtue, did not share the Greek notion of character development, and did not define happiness as their goal. The major differences between the philosophers and Christians therefore reside in the way religion was thought to be related to ethics and in the different views of human nature that they held.

We should be careful not to assume that the moral instructions of the pagan texts represented the actual moral state or practices of Roman or Greek society any more than that the Christian moral instructions described actual conditions in the churches. Not only do they reflect particular moral-philosophical viewpoints but their aim, quite frequently stated explicitly, was to modify current practice or bring about particular behavior in the face of other alternatives. Homosexuality, for example, was widely practiced and justified; the moralists' negative attitude shows that it was also condemned.

It should by now be obvious that the references in this volume to Christian literature are not to be regarded as identifying exact parallels. Sometimes they are exact parallels, sometimes they are more remote, and they are always selective. They are offered as suggestions for closer examination of how particular traditions or styles may have been appropriated and adapted.

The volume has been organized in the way it has in order to address as many interests as possible, and texts have been selected that illustrate a number of features. Chapters 1, 2, and 3 take up issues that are not sufficiently dealt with by students of early Christianity. That the organization draws attention to where and how moral instruction took place does not mean that the treatment of individual topics is confined to the last chapter; careful use of the cross references and the indexes will locate other places throughout the book where important subjects are treated. Other places where these subjects are discussed in ancient literature can easily be identified by consulting the relevant articles in the *Theological Dictionary of the New Testament*, edited by Gerhard Kittel and Gerhard Friedrich; translated by Geoffrey W. Bromiley, 10 volumes (Grand Rapids: Wm. B. Eerdmans Publishing Co., 1964–1976).

Unless otherwise acknowledged, the translations are my own. I wish to thank my colleague Wayne Meeks, for reducing the number of errors that I have made, and Susan Garrett, for preparing the indexes. My wife, Phyllis, with not quite infinite patience but with undeviating commitment, has introduced me to the word processor, on which the manuscript was prepared; as always I am indebted to her. Finally, I am grateful to those students who through the years have read the moralists with me. To them I dedicate this book.

Sources

References to selections are in boldface type.

ARIUS DIDYMUS (*first century* B.C.) was a philosopher at the court of Augustus. He wrote a philosophic handbook from which Stobaeus, the anthologist (fifth century A.D.), excerpted two long sections on Stoic and Peripatetic ethics. Although he has been described as a Stoic, these fragments show him to have been eclectic. His handbook is important for the light it sheds on the type of moral instruction that used such books, but it is not certain to what extent it was used by later philosophers. **60.**

CICERO (*106–43* B.C.) was a member of a prominent Roman family. He studied rhetoric and philosophy in Rome and Greece. Cicero is celebrated for his works on rhetorical theory and for his own speeches, his extensive correspondence, and his philosophical writings. Determined to give the Romans a philosophic literature, late in life he produced works in which he introduced Greek philosophy to an audience that did not read Greek, and in the process he created a Latin philosophical vocabulary. These writings frequently contain systematic treatments of the subjects he discusses. Cicero was not an original thinker, but was eclectic, with an affinity for Stoic ethics and the Skeptic view that probability rather than certainty was all that could be attained. **64.**

CRATES (*ca. 365–285* B.C.) was converted to Cynicism by Diogenes. He represented a more moderate or "hedonistic" form of the philosophy, in which his wife Hipparchia joined him. Only fragments of his works have survived. It is ironic that this much-beloved man should have had attributed to him letters that represent him as an uncompromising rigorist. These letters were probably written during the first and second centuries A.D. **58, 70.**

DEMETRIUS OF PHALERUM (*fourth century* B.C.), a statesman and man of letters, is known mainly for his work on oratory and literary criticism. We know relatively little about his own writings on these subjects, but his name was attached to later works on style which have been preserved. One of these is a handbook on the proper styles to adopt in writing letters. The handbook went through different editions as it in turn sought to influence practice by formulating epistolary theory, and it was itself influenced by the practice that actually resulted. In its present form it likely dates from around the beginning of the Christian era. **32.**

DIO CHRYSOSTOM (A.D. *40–after 112*) was a Greek orator and popular Stoic philosopher from Prusa in Bithynia. He was a student of Musonius Rufus. Banished by Domitian, during his exile he adopted the Cynic way of life, and his discourses from this part of his career are valuable sources for our knowledge of Cynicism. After the death of Domitian he returned to public life and frequently delivered discourses shot through with stock Stoic themes to large audiences. His speeches also provide us with insight into the popular morality and customs of the time. **1, 2, 11, 16, 20, 45, 57, 61, 67.**

DIOGENES (*ca. 400–ca. 325* B.C.) of Sinope in Bithynia gained notoriety while living in Athens and Corinth. The opinion of some ancient as well as modern writers, that he rather than Antisthenes was the founder of Cynicism, may not be true, but he was the first member of the sect to adopt the extravagantly simple mode of life associated with Cynicism. Highly individualistic in his repudiation of the customs and institutions of society, soon after his death he became the subject of numerous anecdotes. The letters attributed to him date from the first century B.C. to the third century A.D., and for the most part represent the extremely rigoristic brand of Cynicism. **12, 18, 43.**

DIOGENES LAERTIUS (*probably early third century* A.D.) was the author of a compendium of the lives and teachings of the ancient philosophers. He made extensive use of earlier summaries and collections of philosophers' teachings in his effort to give an account of Greek philosophy from Thales to Epicurus. **7, 41a, 41b, 41c.**

EPICTETUS (*ca.* A.D. *55–ca. 135*), a former slave, was a student of Musonius Rufus. Like Musonius, in the instruction that he gave young men who were preparing for public life he stressed the ethical teaching of Stoicism. His lectures or diatribes were taken down by Arrian, who, while preserving the style of Epictetus, nevertheless left his own mark on them. There also exists a short manual of Epictetus' principal teachings. **10, 28, 49, 52, 59, 69.**

EPICURUS (*341–270* B.C.) founded a school in Athens in 306 B.C. to compete with other philosophical schools. Called the Garden, from the garden of the house he bought to accommodate the philosophic community he gathered around himself, the school became notorious for its misunderstood teachings on the gods and on pleasure as the only good, and for admitting women. Most of his numerous writings have been lost. *The Principal Doctrines,* a collection of forty moral maxims, is preserved by Diogenes Laertius. **37.**

The *Gnomologium Vaticanum* is a collection of philosophic maxims contained in a fourteenth-century Vatican manuscript. Many of these maxims appear in almost identical form in other collections and in summary accounts of philosophers' doctrines and lives. They enjoyed wide currency early in the Christian era. **39.**

HIEROCLES (*early second century* A.D.), a Stoic writer of dubious originality, is known from two sources: extracts from a philosophic handbook on ethics, preserved by Stobaeus, and a papyrus copy of an elementary introduction to ethics. It is not certain whether these fragments belong to the same or to different works. The extracts from the handbook have proved to be of great importance to the study of popular Stoic morality in general, and the New Testament lists of duties of the members of a household (the so-called *Haustafeln*) in particular. **36.**

HORACE (*65–8* B.C.), the son of a freedman, studied in Rome and Greece, and gained admission to the highest literary and artistic circles in Rome. Of his writings, which include poetry, letters, and satire, the latter two especially reveal the circumstances, aspirations, and failures of people in Roman society. **42.**

ISOCRATES (*436–338* B.C.) was an important Athenian orator. *To Demonicus,* which may originally have been a letter, although attributed to him, was probably written in the fourth century B.C. by a member of his school. **50.**

JULIAN (A.D. *331–363*) is known as the Apostate, for he renounced Christianity and as emperor sought to restore the old paganism. His orations on the philosophers incorporate sources from the second century of the era. **9, 13.**

LUCIAN OF SAMOSATA *(b. ca.* A.D. *120)* was a satirist, sometimes given to caricature, who commented on the foibles of society, especially on the philosophers who would reform it without having reformed themselves. **14, 22, 23, 54.**

MAXIMUS OF TYRE *(ca.* A.D. *125–185)* was an orator who selected philosophic subjects as the themes of his speeches. Although he called himself a Platonist and his speeches on occasion do represent Platonic doctrine, he was no purist but made frequent use of Cynicism and Stoicism. His speeches, which were evidently designed to entertain as well as improve his audiences, assume a level of education found in the salons of the well-to-do where they were delivered. They contain fewer diatribal features than the discourses of Musonius Rufus and Epictetus. **31, 63.**

MELISSA was the name used by Neopythagoreans of chaste persons and beings, and its use in the letter written in her name, dating from between 100 B.C. and A.D. 100, may therefore be symbolic. Nothing is known of a historical Pythagorean woman by this name. **34.**

MUSONIUS RUFUS *(first century* A.D.) was the Stoic teacher of Epictetus and Dio Chrysostom. His lectures on popular moral topics are examples of one style of the diatribe. They are frequently organized around the four cardinal virtues, and were taken down by his student Lucius, whose own style may be discerned in the fragments that have been preserved by Stobaeus. Although Musonius approximates the Cynics in his austere views on what constitutes proper food, clothing, and shelter, his views on slavery, women, marriage, and children are among the most humane of the age in which he lived. **5, 6, 15, 53, 65, 66.**

OXYRHYNCHUS PAPYRUS *115 (second century* A.D.) is named for Oxyrhynchus, an important city in ancient Egypt. The papyrus documents discovered there by modern excavators illuminate the private as well as the public lives of its citizens. **33.**

PLINY THE YOUNGER *(ca.* A.D. *61–ca. 112),* nephew of Pliny the Elder, eventually became governor of Bithynia. He is best known for his letters, which have been preserved in ten books. Nine of these contain true literary epistles, written with careful attention to composition and style, to his friends. After they had been further polished, they were published for the public book trade. The tenth book contains primarily the correspondence between Pliny and Trajan while he served as Trajan's legate in the East. **55.**

PLUTARCH *(before* A.D. *50–after 120),* in later life a priest of Apollo at Delphi and a holder of a municipal office at Chaeronea, where he was born, was a prolific writer. Each of his twenty-three pairs of "Parallel Lives" sketches the life of a famous Greek and a famous Roman, to which he added a short comparison of the two. Eighty-three essays, the "Moralia," include discussions of moral topics, treatises on religion, philosophy, physics, and literature. Plutarch reflects the broad interest of his day in ethical matters, and his writings are major sources for knowledge of first- and second-century culture. While his own philosophic inclination was Platonic, he used traditions from Stoicism and Cynicism that had become common property. His polemical tractates against the Stoics and the Epicureans, however, show that he was not indiscriminately eclectic. **4, 19, 21, 24, 30, 38, 44, 46, 56, 68.**

The Pythagorean Sentences are a collection of moral maxims, dating from the early centuries of the Christian era. They reflect Neopythagorean ethics and piety. **40.**

SENECA *(ca. 4* B.C.–A.D. *65)* was a Roman aristocrat, the son of the rhetorician, the Elder Seneca. He was first tutor and then political adviser to Nero. He was a prolific writer, and his works are a major source for our knowledge of the Stoicism of his time as well as the Cynicism of his friend Demetrius. His letters, written to his friend Lucilius, reveal what issues occupied reflective persons in the first century and are examples of a philosopher's "pastoral" method. **3, 17, 25, 26, 27, 29, 47, 48, 51, 62, 71.**

SEXTUS EMPIRICUS *(late second century* A.D.) was a physician and a Skeptic. His works are major sources for Skepticism's criticism, especially in its later phase, of the "dogmatic" philosophers. **8.**

THEANO was described in antiquity as either Pythagoras' wife or his student Brontinus' wife or daughter. Various positions in the Pythagorean circle as well as a number of writings were attributed to her. The letter to Eubule was written in her name in the first or second century A.D. **35.**

1

The Social Settings
of Moral Instruction

Moral instruction was given in a wide variety of contexts in the Greco-Roman world. The concern with the moral qualities of all persons involved in the nurture and education of children from birth through the various stages of education is illustrated by the tractate *The Education of Children,* attributed to Plutarch (4). In the schools, where the personal example of the teacher was regarded as of major importance (see pp. 135–138), this interest was reflected in the texts chosen for study and in the use of compilations of morally edifying selections from literature (see pp. 115–117), instructive anecdotes and sayings (see pp. 109–115), and, on a more advanced level, systematic summaries of philosophical teachings (see pp. 85–104; **36, 60**).

Christian sources, except for religious instruction in the home (e.g., Eph. 6:4; 2 Tim. 1:5; 3:15), do not reveal a similar preoccupation with the education of children (**35**). Nor does early Christian practice seem to have been public on the same scale. The book of Acts on occasion represents Paul as speaking to the public at large (e.g., Acts 14:8ff.; 17:16ff.) but tends to confine his activity to synagogues (e.g., 13:14ff.; 17:1ff.; 18:4ff.), private homes (e.g., 18:7ff.), or a hall that could have been used by a guild or a school (19:8–10). The stereotyped content of his speeches in these contexts, however, is presented as missionary preaching rather than moral instruction (but see 26:25, where Paul speaks, literally, "words of truth and prudence"). What we do know about Christian moral teaching is derived from literature addressed to churches and not the public. The churches' discussions of morals, based on these documents, may have approximated contemporary school activity.

1   Dio Chrysostom, in introducing himself to an audience **(1)** in
Alexandria and aware of some popular attitudes toward
philosophers, lists the main types of persons who claimed to
engage in moral instruction of the populace at large and concludes with a description, given in antithetic form ("not . . .
but"; cf. 1 Thess. 2:1–8), of the ideal, which he claims to
represent. Some philosophers (e.g., Musonius Rufus and Epictetus) confined themselves to their own schools, others (e.g.,
Maximus of Tyre) attached themselves to aristocratic
households or the imperial court (e.g., Seneca), and a few so
despaired of the human condition **(18)** that they withdrew from
society but still attracted hearers. The majority, however, for
motives noble and otherwise, spoke in public settings ranging
from the forum to the workshop.

Dio Chrysostom, *Oration* 32.7–12

But you have no such critic, neither chorus nor poet nor
anyone else, to reprove you in all friendliness and to reveal
the weaknesses of your city. Therefore, whenever the thing
does at last appear, you should receive it gladly and make a
festival of the occasion instead of being vexed; and even if
vexed, you should be ashamed to call out, "When will the
fellow stop?" or "When is a juggler coming on?" or "Rub-
bish!" or some such thing. For, as I have said, that sort of
entertainment you always have in stock and there is no fear
that it will ever fail you; but discourses like this of mine,
which make men happier and better and more sober and
better able to administer effectively the cities in which they
dwell, you have not often heard—for I do not care to say that
you would not listen to them.

And perhaps this situation is not of your making, but you
will show whether it is or not if you bear with me today; the
fault may lie rather at the door of those who wear the name
of philosopher. For some among that company do not appear in public at all and prefer not to make the venture,
possibly because they despair of being able to improve the
masses; others exercise their voices in what we call lecture-
halls, having secured as hearers men who are in league with
them and tractable. And as for the Cynics, as they are called,
it is true that the city contains no small number of that sect,
and that, like any other thing, this too has had its crop—
persons whose tenets, to be sure, comprise practically noth-

ing spurious or ignoble, yet who must make a living—still these Cynics, posting themselves at street-corners, in alley-ways, and at temple-gates, pass around the hat and play upon the credulity of lads and sailors and crowds of that sort, stringing together rough jokes and much tittle-tattle and that low badinage that smacks of the market-place. Accord-ingly they achieve no good at all, but rather the worst possi-ble harm, for they accustom thoughtless people to deride philosophers in general, just as one might accustom lads to scorn their teachers, and, when they ought to knock the insolence out of their hearers, these Cynics merely increase it.

Those, however, who do come before you as men of cul-ture either declaim speeches intended for display, and stu-pid ones to boot, or else chant verses of their own composi-tion, as if they had detected in you a weakness for poetry. To be sure, if they themselves are really poets or orators, per-haps there is nothing so shocking in that, but if in the guise of philosophers they do these things with a view to their own profit and reputation, and not to improve you, that indeed is shocking. For it is as if a physician when visiting patients should disregard their treatment and their restoration to health, and should bring them flowers and courtesans and perfume.

But there are only a few who have displayed frankness in your presence, and that but sparingly, not in such a way as to fill your ears therewith nor for any length of time; nay, they merely utter a phrase or two, and then, after berating rather than enlightening you, they make a hurried exit, anx-ious lest before they have finished you may raise an outcry and send them packing, behaving in very truth quite like men who in winter muster up courage for a brief and hurried voyage out to sea. But to find a man who in plain terms and without guile speaks his mind with frankness, and neither for the sake of reputation nor for gain makes false pretensions, but out of good will and concern for his fellow-men stands ready, if need be, to submit to ridicule and the disorder of the mob—to find such a man as that is not easy, but rather the good fortune of a very lucky city, so great is the dearth of noble, independent souls and such the abundance of toadies, mountebanks, and sophists.

In my own case, for instance, I feel that I have chosen that rôle, not of my own volition, but by the will of some deity.

For when divine providence is at work for men, the gods provide, not only good counsellors who need no urging, but also words that are appropriate and profitable to the listener.

2   In the face of intense competition, philosophers took great pains to justify their respective methods and arenas of operation by contrasting themselves to their competitors. Dio Chrysostom for a time adopted the Cynic way of life. His account of Diogenes' behavior during the popular Isthmian games, which were held near Corinth and were attended by all kinds of festivities, is designed to commend his own Cynic role as the moral athlete (cf. 1 Cor. 9:24–27; Phil. 3:14; 2 Tim. 2:5; 4:7f.; Heb. 12:1) who seeks out the crowds. By overcoming hardships (see pp. 141–143; cf. Heb. 10:32f.), he strives for virtue rather than the athletes' prizes of parsley, olive, and pine (cf. James 1:12).

Dio Chrysostom, *Oration* 8.4–5, 9–16

4–5. After Antisthenes' death [Diogenes] moved to Corinth, since he considered none of the others worth associating with, and there he lived without renting a house or staying with a friend, but camping out in the Craneion. For he observed that large numbers gathered at Corinth on account of the harbours and the hetaerae, and because the city was situated as it were at the cross-roads of Greece. Accordingly, just as the good physician should go and offer his services where the sick are most numerous, so, said he, the man of wisdom should take up his abode where fools are thickest in order to convict them of their folly and reprove them.

9–16. That was the time, too, when one could hear crowds of wretched sophists around Poseidon's temple shouting and reviling one another, and their disciples, as they were called, fighting with one another, many writers reading aloud their stupid works, many poets reciting their poems while others applauded them, many jugglers showing their tricks, many fortune-tellers interpreting fortunes, lawyers innumerable perverting judgment, and peddlers not a few peddling whatever they happened to have. Naturally a crowd straightway gathered about him too; no Corinthians, however, for they did not think it would be at all worth their while, since they were accustomed to see him every day in Corinth. The crowd that gathered was composed of strangers, and each of these, after speaking or listening for a short time, went his way, fearing his refutation of their views. Just for that reason, said Diogenes, he was like the Laconian dogs; there were plenty of men to pat them and play with them when they were shown at the popular gatherings, but no one was willing to buy any because he did not know how to deal with them.

And when a certain man asked whether he too came to see the contest, he said, "No, but to take part." Then when the man laughed and asked him who his competitors were, he said with that customary glance of his: "The toughest there are and the hardest to beat, men whom no Greek can look straight in the eye; not competitors, however, who sprint or wrestle or jump, not those that box, throw the spear, and hurl the discus, but those that chasten a man." "Who are they, pray?" asked the other. "Hardships," he replied, "very severe and insuperable for gluttonous and folly-stricken men who feast the livelong day and snore at night, but which yield to thin, spare men, whose waists are more pinched in than those of wasps. Or do you think those pot-bellies are good for anything?—creatures whom sensible people ought to lead around, subject to the ceremony of purification, and then thrust beyond the borders, or, rather, kill, quarter, and use as food just as people do with the flesh of large fish, don't you know, boiling it in brine and melting out the fat, the way our people at home in Pontus do with the lard of pigs when they want to anoint themselves. For I think these men have less soul than hogs. But the noble man holds his hardships to be his greatest antagonists, and with them he is ever wont to battle day and night, not to win a sprig of parsley as so many goats might do, nor for a bit of wild olive, or of pine, but to win happiness and virtue throughout all the days of his life, and not merely when the Eleans make proclamation, or the Corinthians, or the Thessalian assembly. He is afraid of none of those opponents nor does he pray to draw another antagonist, but challenges them one after another, grappling with hunger and cold, withstanding thirst, and disclosing no weakness even though he must endure the lash or give his body to be cut or burned. Hunger, exile, loss of reputation, and the like have no terrors for him; nay, he holds them as mere trifles, and while in their very grip the perfect man is often as sportive as boys with their dice and their coloured balls."

3   Seneca, the court philosopher, distinguishes himself from Cynics such as Diogenes (2), and justifies his discrimination in teaching only certain individuals on two grounds: only those who are capable of being improved (see pp. 40–46) should be taught, and the teacher should beware lest he be compromised by persons of inferior character. Still, he should not be hasty in withdrawing from those he regards as hopeless (contrast Gal. 6:1–5; cf. 2 Thess. 3:14f.; Titus 3:8–10).

Seneca, *Epistle* 29.1–7

You have been inquiring about our friend Marcellinus and you desire to know how he is getting along. He seldom comes to see me, for no other reason than that he is afraid to hear the truth, and at present he is removed from any danger of hearing it; for one must not talk to a man unless he is willing to listen. That is why it is often doubted whether Diogenes and the other Cynics, who employed an undiscriminating freedom of speech and offered advice to any who came in their way, ought to have pursued such a plan. For what if one should chide the deaf or those who are speechless from birth or by illness? But you answer: "Why should I spare words? They cost nothing. I cannot know whether I shall help the man to whom I give advice; but I know well that I shall help someone if I advise many. I must scatter this advice by the handful. It is impossible that one who tries often should not sometime succeed."

This very thing, my dear Lucilius, is, I believe, exactly what a great-souled man ought not to do; his influence is weakened; it has too little effect upon those whom it might have set right if it had not grown so stale. The archer ought not to hit the mark only sometimes; he ought to miss it only sometimes. That which takes effect by chance is not an art. Now wisdom is an art; it should have a definite aim; choosing only those who will make progress, but withdrawing from those whom it has come to regard as hopeless,—yet not abandoning them too soon, and just when the case is becoming hopeless trying drastic remedies.

As to our friend Marcellinus, I have not yet lost hope. He

can still be saved, but the helping hand must be offered soon. There is indeed danger that he may pull his helper down; for there is in him a native character of great vigour, though it is already inclining to wickedness. Nevertheless I shall brave this danger and be bold enough to show him his faults. He will act in his usual way; he will have recourse to his wit,—the wit that can call forth smiles even from mourners. He will turn the jest, first against himself, and then against me. He will forestall every word which I am about to utter. He will quiz our philosophic systems; he will accuse philosophers of accepting doles, keeping mistresses, and indulging their appetites. He will point out to me one philosopher who has been caught in adultery, another who haunts the cafés, and another who appears at court.

2

The Aims and Character
of the Moral Teacher

THE GOAL OF PHILOSOPHY

The aims of philosophy in moral teaching were quite practical, such as knowing the right thing to do and what one's responsibilities in social relationships were. It was especially Stoicism that contributed to this view of philosophy as a moral educator, but philosophers did not all define the goal of philosophy in precisely the same way, nor did they all have the same confidence in philosophy as a moral guide. While Jews and Christians put to their own use much of what they found in philosophic practice and teaching, they nevertheless grounded their morality in their religion.

4   The practical concerns of philosophy are well illustrated by this Stoic-influenced tractate which has been attributed erroneously to Plutarch. The list of social duties is a summary of much more extensive treatments, such as that of Hierocles (see pp. 85–104; cf. **60**).

Pseudo-Plutarch, *The Education of Children* **7DE**

Wherefore it is necessary to make philosophy as it were the head and front of all education. For as regards the care of the body men have discovered two sciences, the medical and the gymnastic, of which the one implants health, the other sturdiness, in the body; but for the illnesses and affections of the mind philosophy alone is the remedy. For through philosophy and in company with philosophy it is possible to attain knowledge of what is honourable and what is shameful, what is just and what is unjust, what, in brief, is to be

chosen and what is to be avoided, how a man must bear
himself in his relations with the gods, with his parents, with
his elders, with the laws, with strangers, with those in authority, with friends, with women, with children, with servants;
that one ought to reverence the gods, to honour one's parents, to respect one's elders, to be obedient to the laws, to
yield to those in authority, to love one's friends, to be chaste
with women, to be affectionate with children, and not to
be overbearing with slaves; and, most important of all,
not to be overjoyful at success or overmuch distressed at
misfortune, nor to be dissolute in pleasures, nor impul-
sive and brutish in temper. These things I regard as preeminent among all the advantages which accrue from philosophy.

5   Musonius illustrates how philosophy was also thought to be
effective in personal ethics. He expresses the general conviction that philosophy educates one away from the passions toward self-control or the sober life (cf. Titus 2:11, 12). It was
a common notion among philosophers that the king should
embody the ideal human qualities.

**Musonius Rufus, *Fragment 8 (That Kings Also Should Study
Philosophy)***

In the next place it is essential for the king to exercise self-
control over himself and demand self-control of his subjects,
to the end that with sober rule and seemly submission there
shall be no wantonness on the part of either. For the ruin of
the ruler and the citizen alike is wantonness. But how would
anyone achieve self-control if he did not make an effort to
curb his desires, or how could one who is undisciplined
make others temperate? One can mention no study except
philosophy that develops self-control. Certainly it teaches
one to be above pleasure and greed, to admire thrift and to
avoid extravagance; it trains one to have a sense of shame,
and to control one's tongue, and it produces discipline,
order, and courtesy, and in general what is fitting in action
and in bearing. In an ordinary man when these qualities are
present they give him dignity and self-command, but if they
be present in a king they make him preeminently godlike and
worthy of reverence.

6   According to Musonius, the divine endows all people with
reason, and the philosophic life is not reserved for specialists
or professionals. It is the divine will (cf. Rom. 12:2; Eph. 5:
15–17; 1 Thess. 4:3; 1 Peter 2:15) that we take up philosophy
and thus become good. It is therefore appropriate to exhort
someone to do so as Musonius does here, in this case a young
man **(22, 23)**.

Musonius Rufus, *Fragment* **16** *(What Is the Best Provision for
Old Age?)*

> If, then, my young friend, with a view to becoming such a
> man, as you surely will if you truly master the lessons of
> philosophy, you should not be able to induce your father to
> permit you to do as you wish, nor succeed in persuading
> him, reason thus: your father forbids you to study philoso-
> phy, but the common father of all men and gods, Zeus, bids
> you and exhorts you to do so. His command and law is that
> man be just and honest, beneficent, temperate, high-
> minded, superior to pain, superior to pleasure, free of all
> envy and malice; to put it briefly, the law of Zeus bids man
> be good. But being good is the same as being a philosopher.
> If you obey your father, you will follow the will of a man; if
> you choose the philosopher's life, the will of God. It is plain,
> therefore, that your duty lies in the pursuit of philosophy
> rather than not. But, you say, your father will restrain you
> and actually shut you up to prevent your study of philoso-
> phy. Perhaps he will do so, but he will not prevent you from
> studying philosophy unless you are willing; for we do not
> study philosophy with our hands and feet or any other part
> of the body, but with the soul and with a very small part of
> it, that which we call the reason. This God placed in the
> strongest place so that it might be inaccessible to sight and
> touch, free from all compulsion and in its own power. Partic-
> ularly if your mind is good your father will not be able to
> prevent you from using it nor from thinking what you ought
> nor from liking the good and not liking the base; nor again
> from choosing the one and rejecting the other. In the very
> act of doing this, you would be studying philosophy, and you
> would not need to wrap yourself up in a worn cloak nor go
> without a chiton nor grow long hair nor deviate from the
> ordinary practices of the average man. To be sure, such
> things are well enough for professional philosophers, but

philosophy does not consist in them, but rather in thinking out what is man's duty and meditating upon it.

7   This extract from a letter of Epicurus is similar to the preceding selection in not confining protrepsis (exhortation to take up the philosophic life) to any particular age or circumstance. What was characteristic of the Epicureans, however, was their stress on pleasure in defining happiness as the goal of philosophy.

Diogenes Laertius, *Lives of Eminent Philosophers* 10.122

Let no one be slow to seek wisdom when he is young nor weary in the search thereof when he is grown old. For no age is too early or too late for the health of the soul. And to say that the season for studying philosophy has not yet come, or that it is past and gone, is like saying that the season for happiness is not yet or that it is now no more. Therefore, both old and young ought to seek wisdom, the former in order that, as age comes over him, he may be young in good things because of the grace of what has been, and the latter in order that, while he is young, he may at the same time be old, because he has no fear of the things which are to come. So we must exercise ourselves in the things which bring happiness, since, if that be present, we have everything, and, if that be absent, all our actions are directed toward attaining it.

8   The Skeptics represented a minority viewpoint. The contradictions they delighted in pointing out in the claims of scientific philosophers (the "dogmatists") led them to a suspension of judgment in matters of doctrine. In moral matters, they held that tranquillity is attained by moderation and living according to established custom and law.

Sextus Empiricus, *Outlines of Pyrrhonism* 3.235–238

Accordingly, the Sceptic, seeing so great a diversity of usages, suspends judgement as to the natural existence of anything good or bad or (in general) fit or unfit to be done, therein abstaining from the rashness of dogmatism; and he follows undogmatically the ordinary rules of life, and because of this he remains impassive in respect of matters of opinion, while in conditions that are necessitated his emotions are moderate; for though, as a human being, he suffers emotion through his senses, yet because he does not also opine that what he suffers is evil by nature, the emotion he suffers is moderate. For the added opinion that a thing is of such a kind is worse than the actual suffering itself, just as sometimes the patients themselves bear a surgical operation, while the bystanders swoon away because of their opinion that it is a horrible experience. But, in fact, he who assumes that there exists by nature something good or bad or, generally, fit or unfit to be done, is disquieted in various ways. For when he experiences what he regards as natural evils he deems himself to be pursued by Furies, and when he becomes possessed of what seems to him good things he falls into no ordinary state of disquiet both through arrogance and through fear of losing them, and through trying to guard against finding himself again amongst what he regards as natural evils; for those who assert that goods are incapable of being lost we shall put to silence by means of the doubts raised by their dissension. Hence we conclude that if what is productive of evil is evil and to be shunned, and the persuasion that these things are good, those evil, by nature produces disquiet, then the assumption and persuasion that anything is, in its real nature, either bad or good is evil and to be shunned.

THE PHILOSOPHER AND HIS TASK

BEGINS WITH HIMSELF

Philosophers frequently found it necessary to justify their activity as moral reformers. Given the practical and nontechnical nature of much of philosophy, during the first and second centuries A.D. large numbers of charlatans for their own profit invaded the cities. Lucian's *The Runaways* provides a vivid description. Genuine philosophers developed a manner of self-description that contrasted themselves to their competitors (1), clarified their motivations, and asserted their superiority over the majority of people.

9   The rigorous self-examination required before daring to correct others is summarized by Julian (cf. *1 Clem.* 7.1; Polycarp, *Phil.* 4.1) in terms of three common vices: pleasure of the body, money, and reputation (16, 57). Only after he had freed him-

self from them could the philosopher, on the basis of that attainment, engage in frank speech designed to benefit the people who listened to him (cf. 1 Tim. 4:11–16; Titus 3:7–8; contrast 1 Cor. 3:18; 4:17; Phil. 3:4–13). In his description of the ideal Cynic, Julian uses earlier sources.

Julian, *Oration* 6.200C–201C

But let me go back to what I said before, that he who is entering on the career of a Cynic ought first to censure severely and cross-examine himself, and without any self-flattery ask himself the following questions in precise terms: whether he enjoys expensive food; whether he cannot do without a soft bed; whether he is the slave of rewards and the opinion of men; whether it is his ambition to attract public notice and even though that be an empty honour he still thinks it worth while. Nevertheless he must not let himself drift with the current of the mob or touch vulgar pleasure even with the tip of his finger, as the saying is, until he has succeeded in trampling on it; then and not before he may permit himself to dip into that sort of thing if it come his way. For instance I am told that bulls which are weaker than the rest separate themselves from the herd and pasture alone while they store up their strength in every part of their bodies by degrees, until they rejoin the herd in good condition, and then they challenge its leaders to contend with them, in confidence that they are more fit to take the lead. Therefore let him who wishes to be a Cynic philosopher not adopt merely their long cloak or wallet or staff or their way of wearing the hair, as though he were like a man walking unshaved and illiterate in a village that lacked barbers' shops and schools, but let him consider that reason rather than a staff and a certain plan of life rather than a wallet are the mintmarks of the Cynic philosophy. And freedom of speech he must not employ until he have first proved how much he is worth, as I believe was the case with Crates and Diogenes. For they were so far from bearing with a bad grace any threat of fortune, whether one call such threats caprice or wanton insult, that once when he had been captured by pirates Diogenes joked with them; as for Crates he gave his property to the state, and being physically deformed he made fun of his own lame leg and hunched shoulders. But when his friends gave an entertainment he used to go, whether invited or not,

and would reconcile his nearest friends if he learned that
they had quarreled. He used to reprove them not harshly
but with a charming manner and not so as to seem to perse-
cute those whom he wished to reform, but as though he
wished to be of use both to them and to the bystanders.

10 Epictetus, in the popular philosophic style known as diatribe,
in which dialogue is used (see pp. 129–134), demonstrates how
his ideal philosopher might carry out such a self-examination
(**62**). His picture of the philosopher is Stoic; hence there is a
strong emphasis on the philosopher finding himself in the
divine scheme of things. Certain that he performs his role in
accord with the providential order of things (**1**; cf. Rom. 1:1;
1 Cor. 1:1; Gal. 1:15), the philosopher describes himself as
God's messenger and scout. Sent by God, the ideal sage cannot be hidden but presents himself as a paradigm of virtuous
attainment.

Epictetus, *Discourse* 3.22.38–49

"In what, then, is the good, since it is not in these things?
Tell us, Sir messenger and scout." "It is where you do not
expect it, and do not wish to look for it. For if you had
wished, you would have found it within you, and you would
not now be wandering outside, nor would you be seeking
what does not concern you, as though it were your own
possession. Turn your thoughts upon yourselves, find out
the kind of preconceived ideas which you have. What sort of
thing do you imagine the good to be? Serenity, happiness,
freedom from restraint. Come, do you not imagine it to be
something naturally great? Something precious? Something
not injurious? In what kind of subject matter for life ought
one to seek serenity, and freedom from restraint? In that
which is slave, or that which is free?" "In the free." "Is the
paltry body which you have, then, free or is it a slave?" "We
know not." "You do not know that it is a slave of fever, gout,
ophthalmia, dysentery, a tyrant, fire, iron, everything that is
stronger?" "Yes, it is their servant." "How, then, can anything that pertains to the body be unhampered? And how
can that which is naturally lifeless, earth, or clay, be great or
precious? What then? Have you nothing that is free?" "Perhaps nothing." "And who can compel you to assent to that
which appears to you to be false?" "No one." "And who to

refuse assent to that which appears to you to be true?" "No one." "Here, then, you see that there is something within you which is naturally free. But to desire, or to avoid, or to choose, or to refuse, or to prepare, or to set something before yourself—what man among you can do these things without first conceiving an impression of what is profitable, or what is not fitting?" "No one." "You have, therefore, here too, something unhindered and free. Poor wretches, develop this, pay attention to this, seek here your good."

And how is it possible for a man who has nothing, who is naked, without home or hearth, in squalor, without a slave, without a city to live serenely? Behold, God has sent you the man who will show in practice that it is possible. "Look at me," he says, "I am without a home, without a city, without property, without a slave; I sleep on the ground; I have neither wife nor children, no miserable governor's mansion, but only earth, and sky, and one rough cloak. Yet what do I lack? Am I not free from pain and fear, am I not free? When has anyone among you seen me failing to get what I desire, or falling into what I would avoid? When have I ever found fault with either God or man? When have I ever blamed anyone? Has anyone among you seen me with a gloomy face? And how do I face those persons before whom you stand in fear and awe? Do I not face them as slaves? Who, when he lays eyes upon me, does not feel that he is seeing his king and his master?"

11 Having risen to such heights, the wise man needs no one, for he has demonstrated his superiority to the whole world (**20**; contrast 1 Cor. 15:8–10; Gal. 1:11–17; Phil. 3:4–11; 1 Tim. 1:12–17).

Dio Chrysostom, *Oration* 49.8–11

And indeed it is reasonable to expect that man to administer any office most capably who, occupying continuously the most difficult office of all, can show himself to be free from error. For example, the philosopher is always master of himself; and this is altogether more difficult than to be king over all the Greeks or all the barbarians. For what race of men is as savage as are anger and envy and contentiousness, things over which the philosopher must maintain control? What race is as knavish and intriguing and traitorous as are pleasures and lusts, by which he must never be overcome? What race is as violent and terrifying and debasing to men's souls as are fear and pain, to which he must never be seen to yield? Again, what armour, what defences does he possess for protection against these forces such as both kings and generals have against a foe? What allies or bodyguards can he employ against them, unless it be words of wisdom and prudence? Whom else can he bid do sentry duty or trust to stand guard, or what servants can he employ? Is he not, on the contrary, obliged to hold this watch himself both night and day, with anxious thought and vigilance, lest, ere he is aware of it, he may be excited by pleasures or terrified by fears or tricked by lust or brought low by pain and so be made to abandon those acts which are best and most righteous, turning traitor to himself? However, the man who administers this office with firmness and self-control does not find it difficult from then on to show himself superior to even the whole world.

CONFORMITY OF SPEECH TO LIFE

The common wisdom that one's speech should agree with one's deeds (cf. Matt. 23:3; Rom. 2:1, 21–23; 1 John 3:18; *1 Clem.* 30.3; Ignatius, *Eph.* 15.1) was particularly applied to philosophers who justified their exhortation by their own moral progress or attainment.

12 The philosophers' entire manner of life, extending in the case of Cynics to their simple garb, could be pointed to as a deliberate demonstration of the principles they taught (cf. Rom. 15: 18).

Pseudo-Diogenes, *Epistle* 15

I hear that you say I am doing nothing unusual in wearing a double, ragged cloak and carrying a wallet. Now I admit that none of these is extraordinary, but each of them is good when undertaken out of conscious determination. For not only is it necessary that the body exercise this simplicity, but the spirit should too, along with it. That is to say, it should not promise much and then do what is not sufficient, but should demonstrate that the spoken claims conform to the way of life. In fact, it is this that I try to do and witness in my case. Will you perhaps take me to be speaking of the people of Athens or Corinth as unjust witnesses? I am speaking of my own spirit, whose notice I cannot escape when I do wrong.

13 The ancient Cynics, who valued deeds more than words, were on occasion presented as offering ideal examples in this respect (cf. James 3:13; *2 Clem.* 4; see pp. 135–138).

Julian, *Oration* 7.214BCD

Now what was the manner of Cynics' association with people? Deeds with them came before words, and if they honoured poverty they themselves seem first to have scorned inherited wealth; if they cultivated modesty, they themselves first practised plain living in every respect; if they tried to expel from the lives of other men the element of theatrical display and arrogance, they themselves first set the example by living in the open market places and the temple precincts, and they opposed luxury by their own practice before they did so in words; nor did they shout aloud but proved by their actions that a man may rule as the equal of Zeus if he needs nothing or very little and so is not hampered by his body; and they reproved sinners during the lifetime of those who offended but did not speak ill of the dead; for when men are dead even their enemies, at least the more moderate, make peace with the departed.

14 It is not surprising that a favorite means of attacking philosophers was to accuse them of inconsistency between their speech and behavior (cf. Paul's self-defense, 2 Cor. 10:11).

Lucian, *Icaromenippus* 29–31

There is a class of men which made its appearance in the world not long ago, lazy, disputatious, vainglorious, quick-tempered, gluttonous, doltish, addle-pated, full of effrontery and to use the language of Homer, "a useless load to the soil" [*Iliad* 18.104]. Well, these people, dividing themselves into schools and inventing various word-mazes, have called themselves Stoics, Academics, Epicureans, Peripatetics and other things much more laughable than these. Then, cloaking themselves in the high-sounding name of Virtue, elevating their eyebrows, wrinkling up their foreheads and

letting their beards grow long, they go about hiding loath-
some habits under a false garb, very like actors in tragedy;
for if you take away from the latter their masks and their
gold-embroidered robes, nothing is left but a comical little
creature hired for the show at seven drachmas.

But although that is what they are, they look with scorn on
all mankind and they tell absurd stories about the gods;
collecting lads who are easy to hoodwink, they rant about
their far-famed "Virtue" and teach them their insoluble fal-
lacies; and in the presence of their disciples they always sing
the praise of restraint and temperance and self-sufficiency
and spit at wealth and pleasure, but when they are all by
themselves, how can one describe how much they eat, how
much they indulge their passions and how they lick the filth
off pennies?

Worst of all, though they themselves do no good either in
public or in private life but are useless and superfluous,
"neither in war nor in council of any account" [Homer, *Iliad*
2.202], nevertheless they accuse everyone else, they amass
biting phrases and school themselves in novel terms of
abuse, and then they censure and reproach their fellow-men;
and whoever of them is the most noisy and impudent and
reckless in calling names is held to be the champion. But if
you were to ask the very man who is straining his lungs and
bawling and accusing everybody else: "How about yourself?
What do you really do, and what in Heaven's name do you
contribute to the world?" he would say, if he were willing to
say what was right and true: "I hold it unnecessary to be a
merchant or a farmer or a soldier or to follow a trade; I
shout, go dirty, take cold baths, walk about barefoot in winter, wear a filthy mantle and like Momus [a literary figure
who personified faultfinding] carp at everything the others
do. If some rich man or other has made an extravagant
outlay on a dinner or keeps a mistress, I make it my affair and
get hot about it; but if one of my friends or associates is ill
abed and needs relief and attendance, I ignore it."

THE HUMAN CONDITION

While the moral philosophers claimed to have made considerable
progress in their own moral growth, they differed widely in their
perceptions of the condition of humanity at large. The most positive
views are expressed by those philosophers who taught in relatively

secluded contexts and the most negative by preachers to the masses. The styles of these moralists, from Seneca's self-conscious, almost academic comments on epistolographic practice and philosophical rhetoric and his penchant for classification, to Musonius' calm argument and the Cynic's tirade, partly correspond to their audiences and the social settings in which they taught.

15   Musonius, a humane philosophical teacher, represents an optimistic view.

Musonius Rufus, *Fragment 2 (That Man Is Born with an Inclination Toward Virtue)*

> All of us, [Rufus] used to say, are so fashioned by nature that we can live our lives free from error and nobly; not that one can and another cannot, but all. The clearest evidence of this is the fact that lawgivers lay down for all alike what may be done and forbid what may not be done, exempting from punishment no one who disobeys or does wrong, not the young nor the old, not the strong nor the weak, not anyone whomsoever. And yet if the whole notion of virtue were something that came to us from without, and we shared no part of it by birth, just as in activities pertaining to the other arts no one who has not learned the art is expected to be free from error, so in like manner in things pertaining to the conduct of life it would not be reasonable to expect anyone to be free from error who had not learned virtue, seeing that virtue is the only thing that saves us from error in daily living. Now in the care of the sick we demand no one but the physician to be free from error, and in handling the lyre no one but the musician, and in managing the helm no one but the pilot, but in the conduct of life it is no longer only the philosopher whom we expect to be free from error, though he alone would seem to be the only one concerned with the study of virtue, but all men alike, including those who have never given any attention to virtue. Clearly, then, there is no explanation for this other than that the human being is born with an inclination toward virtue. And this indeed is strong evidence of the presence of goodness in our nature, that all speak of themselves as having virtue and being good. For take the common man; when asked whether he is stupid or intelligent, not one will confess to being stupid; or again, when asked whether he is just or unjust, not one will say that

he is unjust. In the same way, if one asks him whether he is temperate or intemperate, he replies at once that he is temperate; and finally, if one asks whether he is good or bad, he would say that he is good, even though he can name no teacher of virtue or mention any study or practice of virtue he has ever made. Of what, then, is this evidence if not of an innate inclination of the human soul toward goodness and nobleness, and of the presence of the seeds of virtue in each one of us? Moreover, because it is entirely to our advantage to be good, some of us deceive ourselves into thinking that we are really good, while others of us are ashamed to admit that we are not. Why then, pray, when one who has not learned letters or music or gymnastics never claims to have knowledge of these arts nor makes any pretence of knowing them, and is quite unable even to name a teacher to whom he went, why, I say, does everyone profess that he has virtue? It is because none of those other skills is natural to man, and no human being is born with a natural faculty for them, whereas an inclination toward virtue is inborn in each one of us.

16 Dio Chrysostom, with extensive experience in preaching to the masses behind him, is less positive than his teacher Musonius. Instead of reflecting on the seeds of virtue innate in us all, Dio is more impressed by the majority's helplessness and ignorance, which is assumed by most moralists to be the cause of vicious lives (cf. Acts 17:22–30; 1 Peter 1:13–19; contrast Rom. 1:18–31). Yet Dio is far more optimistic than the misanthropic Cynic who writes under the name of Diogenes (**18**).

Dio Chrysostom, *Oration* **13.13**

And the opinion I had was that pretty well all men are fools, and that no one does any of the things he should do, or considers how to rid himself of the evils that beset him and of his great ignorance and confusion of mind, so as to live a more virtuous and a better life; but that they all are being thrown into confusion and are swept round and round in the same place and about practically the same objects, to wit, money and reputation and certain pleasures of the body, while no one is able to rid himself of these and set his own soul free; just as, I fancy, things that get into a whirlpool are tossed and rolled without being able to free themselves from the whirling.

17   Seneca represents a more scholastic and nuanced Stoic view which grants a prominent place to the notion of progress (cf. 1 Tim. 4:15). Nevertheless, also Stoic is his hesitation to promise that virtue will actually be attained; most people find themselves somewhere between virtue and vice. Seneca's use of medical imagery in discussing the moral condition is common among all moralists (cf. 1 Tim. 6:3–5; 2 Tim. 2:16–17; Titus 1:15). For the treatment of people of different position, see **25;** for the philosopher's speech, see pp. 68–79.

Seneca, *Epistle* 75 *(On the Diseases of the Soul)*

You have been complaining that my letters to you are rather carelessly written. Now who talks carefully unless he also desires to talk affectedly? I prefer that my letters should be just what my conversation would be if you and I were sitting in one another's company or taking walks together,—spontaneous and easy; for my letters have nothing strained or artificial about them. If it were possible, I should prefer to show, rather than speak, my feelings. Even if I were arguing a point, I should not stamp my foot, or toss my arms about, or raise my voice; but I should leave that sort of thing to the orator, and should be content to have conveyed my feelings to you without having either embellished them or lowered their dignity. I should like to convince you entirely of this one fact,—that I feel whatever I say, that I not only feel it, but am wedded to it. It is one sort of kiss which a man gives to his mistress, and another which he gives his children; yet in the father's embrace also, holy and restrained as it is, plenty of affection is disclosed.

I prefer, however, that our conversation on matters so important should not be meagre and dry; for even philosophy does not renounce the company of cleverness. One should not, however, bestow very much attention on mere words. Let this be the kernel of my idea: let us say what we feel, and feel what we say; let speech harmonize with life. That man has fulfilled his promise who is the same person both when you see him and when you hear him. We shall not fail to see what sort of man he is and how large a man he is, if only he is one and the same. Our words should aim not to please, but to help. If, however, you can attain eloquence without painstaking, and if you either are naturally gifted or can gain eloquence at slight cost, make the most of it and apply it to the noblest uses. But let it be of such a kind that it displays facts rather than itself. It and the other arts are wholly concerned with cleverness; but our business here is the soul.

A sick man does not call in a physician who is eloquent; but if it so happens that the physician who can cure him likewise discourses elegantly about the treatment which is to be followed, the patient will take it in good part. For all that, he will not find any reason to congratulate himself on having found a physician who is eloquent. For the case is no different from that of a skilled pilot who is also handsome. Why do you tickle my ears? Why do you entertain me? There is other business at hand; I am to be cauterized, operated upon, or put on a diet. That is why you were summoned to treat me!

You are required to cure a disease that is chronic and serious,—one which affects the general weal. You have as serious a business on hand as a physician has during a plague. Are you concerned about *words*? Rejoice this instant if you can cope with *things*. When shall you learn all that there is to learn? When shall you so plant in your mind that which you have learned, that it cannot escape? When shall you put it all into practice? For it is not sufficient merely to commit these things to memory, like other matters; they must be practically tested. He is not happy who only knows them, but he who does them. You reply: "What? Are there no degrees of happiness below your 'happy' man? Is there a sheer descent immediately below wisdom?" I think not. For though he who makes progress is still numbered with the fools, yet he is separated from them by a long interval. Among the very persons who are making progress there are also great spaces intervening. They fall into three classes, as certain philosophers believe. First come those who have not yet attained wisdom but have already gained a place near by. Yet even that which is not far away is still outside. These, if you ask me, are men who have already laid aside all passions and vices, who have learned what things are to be embraced; but their assurance is not yet tested. They have not yet put their good into practice, yet from now on they cannot slip back into the faults which they had escaped. They have already arrived at a point from which there is no slipping back, but they are not yet aware of the fact; as I remember writing in another letter, "They are ignorant of their knowledge." It has now been vouchsafed to them to enjoy their good, but not yet to be sure of it. Some define this class, of which I have been speaking,—a class of men who are making progress,—as having escaped the diseases of the mind, but not yet the passions, and as still standing upon slippery ground; because no one is beyond the dangers of evil except him who has cleared himself of it wholly. But no one has so cleared himself except the man who has adopted wisdom in its stead.

I have often before explained the difference between the diseases of the mind and its passions. And I shall remind you once more: the diseases are hardened and chronic vices, such as greed and ambition; they have enfolded the mind in too close a grip, and have begun to be permanent evils thereof. To give a brief definition: by "disease" we mean a persistent perversion of the judgment, so that things which are mildly desirable are thought to be highly desirable. Or, if you prefer, we may define it thus: to be too zealous in striving for things which are only mildly desirable or not desirable at all, or to value highly things which ought to be valued but slightly or valued not at all. "Passions" are objectionable impulses of the spirit, sudden and vehement; they have come so often, and so little attention has been paid to them, that they have caused a state of disease; just as a catarrh, when there has been but a single attack and the catarrh has not yet become habitual, produces a cough, but causes consumption when it has become regular and chronic. Therefore we may say that those who have made most progress are beyond the reach of the "diseases"; but they still feel the "passions" even when very near perfection.

The second class is composed of those who have laid aside both the greatest ills of the mind and its passions, but yet are not in assured possession of immunity. For they can still slip back into their former state. The third class are beyond the reach of many of the vices and particularly of the great vices, but not beyond the reach of all. They have escaped avarice, for example, but still feel anger; they no longer are troubled by lust, but are still troubled by ambition; they no longer have desire, but they still have fear. And just because they fear, although they are strong enough to withstand certain things, there are certain things to which they yield; they scorn death, but are in terror of pain.

Let us reflect a moment on this topic. It will be well with us if we are admitted to this class. The second stage is gained by great good fortune with regard to our natural gifts and by great and unceasing application to study. But not even the third type is to be despised. Think of the host of evils which you see about you; behold how there is no crime that is not exemplified, how far wickedness advances every day, and how prevalent are sins in home and commonwealth. You will see, therefore, that we are making a considerable gain, if we are not numbered among the basest.

"But as for me," you say, "I hope that it is in me to rise to a higher rank than that!" I should pray, rather than promise, that we may attain this; we have been forestalled. We hasten towards virtue while hampered by vices. I am ashamed to say it; but we worship that which is honourable only in so far as we have time to spare. But what a rich reward awaits us if only we break off the affairs which forestall us and the evils that cling to us with utter tenacity! Then neither desire nor fear shall rout us. Undisturbed by fears, unspoiled by pleasures, we shall be afraid neither of death nor of the gods; we shall know that death is no evil and that the gods are not powers of evil. That which harms has no greater power than that which receives harm, and things which are utterly good have no power at all to harm. There await us, if ever we escape from these low dregs to that sublime and lofty height, peace of mind and, when all error has been driven out, perfect liberty. You ask what this freedom is? It means not fearing either men or gods; it means not craving wickedness or excess; it means possessing supreme power over oneself. And it is a priceless good to be master of oneself. Farewell.

18 The Cynic who wrote this letter represents the misanthropic wing of his sect who despaired of the human condition and thought gentleness the method of old people and wet nurses (contrast 1 Thess. 2:7; cf. 2 Cor. 10:1). He is considerably harsher even than Dio.

Pseudo-Diogenes, *Epistle* 29.4–5

Poor soul, there is no harsher burden for you than the ways of your forefathers and of the tyrants. There is nothing else which more consistently destroys you. Yet you cannot find a man with this purpose, that he preserve you from the sacred sickness which is also called tyranny. For you do everything that a madman does, although you would be saved if you held back from this alone. However, your companions do not see the extent of your evil, nor do you yourself perceive it, for so long and so thoroughly has the sickness gripped you. Consequently you need a whip and an overlord and not someone who will admire and flatter you. Indeed, how could anyone be benefited by this sort of person, and how would such a person benefit anyone? Only if he chastise him like a horse or an ox and at the same time recall him to his senses and pay heed to what is lacking.

But you are in an advanced stage of corruption. Therefore, cutting, cautery and medication must be employed. But you, like little children, have brought in for yourselves a number of grandparents and wetnurses who say to you, "Here, my child, fill your cup if you love me. Eat just this little bit more." And so, if all men and women assembled and called down curses on you, you couldn't do more to further the disease alone.

3

Methods of Instruction and Moral Nurture

The moral philosophers gave considerable attention to developing methods by which to cultivate moral growth. These methods, which were perpetuated and further developed in later Christian monastic orders, included what we would call psychotherapy, psychological and pastoral counseling, spiritual direction or soul care, and the most general exhortation. The term used to describe this entire range of activity is "psychagogy." While the literature naturally stresses the role of the philosopher (cf. 1 Tim. 4:13; 5:1; 6:2; 2 Tim. 4:2; Ignatius, *Pol.* 1.2) in exhortation, groups such as the Epicureans engaged in exhortation, admonition, and consolation of each other (cf. Rom. 15:14; 1 Thess. 5:12–15; Heb. 3:13; 10:25; *Barn.* 19.4; *1 Clem.* 56.2; *2 Clem.* 17.2; Hermas, *Vis.* 3.9.10). The following examples demonstrate the moralists' genuine concern to benefit their audiences.

INSTRUCTION OF GROUPS AND INDIVIDUALS

Although the impression may be gained that most instruction was of groups, in fact the desirability of personal, individual instruction was widely recognized (cf. Matt. 18:15; Acts 20:31; 1 Thess. 2:11; 5:11). Precisely because the philosopher was to be frank in exposing his friend's errors, Plutarch cautions circumspection and emphasizes the value of private instruction. The goal is always to benefit the other person (cf. Gal. 6:1).

19

Plutarch, *How to Tell a Flatterer from a Friend* 70D–71C

This perhaps was rather severe. But another opportunity for admonition arises when people, having been reviled by others for their errors, have become submissive and downcast. The tactful man will make an adept use of this, by rebuffing and dispersing the revilers, and by taking hold of his friend in private and reminding him that, if there is no other reason for his being circumspect, he should at least try to keep his enemies from being bold. "For where have these fellows a chance to open their mouths, or what can they say against you, if you put away and cast from you all that which gets you a bad name?" In this way he who reviles is charged with hurting, and he who admonishes is credited with helping.

But some persons manage more cleverly, and by finding fault with strangers, turn their own intimate acquaintances to repentance; for they accuse the others of what they know their own acquaintances are doing. My professor, Ammonius, at an afternoon lecture perceived that some of his students had eaten a luncheon that was anything but frugal, and so he ordered his freedman to chastise his own servant, remarking by way of explanation that "that boy can't lunch without his wine!" At the same time he glanced towards us, so that the rebuke took hold of the guilty.

One other point: we must be very careful about the use of frank speech toward a friend before a large company, bearing in mind the incident in which Plato was involved. It so happened that Socrates had handled one of his acquaintances rather severely in a conversation which took place close by the money-changers', whereupon Plato said, "Were it not better that this had been said in private?" Socrates retorted, "Should you not have done better if you had addressed your remark to me in private?" And again, when Pythagoras once assailed a devoted pupil pretty roughly in the presence of several persons, the youth, as the story goes, hanged himself, and from that time on Pythagoras never admonished anybody when anyone else was present. For error should be treated as a foul disease, and all admonition and disclosure should be in secret, with nothing of show or display in it to attract a crowd of witnesses and spectators. For it is not like friendship, but sophistry, to seek for glory in other men's faults, and to make a fair show before the spectators, like the physicians who perform operations in the theatres with an eye to attracting patients. Quite apart from the affront involved—which ought never to be allowed in any corrective treatment—some regard must be paid to the contentiousness and self-will that belong to vice; for it is not enough to say, as Euripides has it [*Stheneboea;* Nauck, *T.G.F.* 665], that "Love reproved more urgent grows," but if admonition be offered in public, and unsparingly, it only confirms each and every morbid emotion in its shamelessness. Hence, just as Plato insists that elderly men who are trying to cultivate a sense of respect among the young, must themselves, first of all, show respect for the young, so among friends a modest frankness best engenders modesty, and a cautious quiet approach and treatment of the erring one saps the foundations of his vice and annihilates it, since it gradually becomes imbued with consideration for the consideration shown to it. It follows, then, that the best way is to "Hold one's head quite close, that the others may not hear it" [Homer, *Odyssey* 1.157]. And least of all is it decent to expose a husband in the hearing of his wife, and a father in the sight of his children, and a lover in the presence of his beloved, or a teacher in the presence of his students: for such persons are driven almost insane with grief and anger at being taken to task before those with whom they feel it is necessary to stand well.

ADAPTATION TO CIRCUMSTANCES

The genuine desire to aid people by one's instruction suggests that the teacher adapt his teaching to the circumstances and conditions of those he would help (cf. 1 Cor. 9:19–23). In the following two selections, Plutarch and Dio adhere to the need for frankness that causes pain, but only insofar as frankness is salutary. Their discussions are marked by their insistence on gentleness, an emphasis that may be seen as a reaction to the harsh Cynics (18) who had identified their own excoriating style as the only proper frank speech (cf. 1 Thess. 2:7; 2 Tim. 2:24–26).

20 Dio Chrysostom mentions some types of persuasion that might be appropriate as particular or individual circumstances are taken into consideration (cf. Acts 20:31; 1 Thess. 2:11; Ignatius, *Pol.* 1.3; 4.2), but he is also aware of the speaker's need to maintain his own integrity while he adapts.

Dio Chrysostom, *Oration* 77/78.37–45

But he who in very truth is manly and high-minded would never submit to any such things, nor would he sacrifice his own liberty and his freedom of speech for the sake of any dishonourable payment of either power or riches, nor would he envy those who change their form and apparel for such rewards; on the contrary, he would think such persons to be comparable to those who change from human beings into snakes or other animals, not envying them, nor yet carping at them because of their wantonness, but rather bewailing and pitying them when they, like the boys, with an eye to gifts have their hair cut off, and grey hair at that! But as for himself, the man of whom I speak will strive to preserve his individuality in seemly fashion and with steadfastness, never deserting his post of duty, but always honouring and promoting virtue and sobriety and trying to lead all men thereto, partly by persuading and exhorting, partly by abusing and reproaching, in the hope that he may thereby rescue somebody from folly and from low desires and intemperance and soft living, taking them aside privately one by one and also admonishing them in groups every time he finds the opportunity, "with gentle words at times, at others harsh" [Homer, *Iliad* 12.267] until, methinks, he shall have spent his life in caring for human beings, not cattle or horses or camels and houses, sound in words and sound in deeds, a safe travelling companion for any one to have on land or sea and a good omen for men to behold when offering sacrifice, not arousing strife or greed or contentions and jealousies and base desires for gain, but reminding men of sobriety and righteousness and promoting concord, but as for insatiate greed and shamelessness and moral weakness, expelling them as best he can—in short, a person far more sacred than the bearers of a truce or the heralds who in times of war come bringing an armistice.

Therefore he wishes, yes, is eager, in so far as he can, to aid all men; though sometimes he is defeated by other men and other practices and has little or no power at all. Finally, he purges his own mind by the aid of reason and tries to render it exempt from slavery, fighting in defence of freedom a much more stubborn battle against lusts and opinions and all mankind, aided by the few who wish to help him, than once the Spartans fought when, having seized the pass, they gave battle to all the hordes from Asia, few though those Spartans were, for three nights and days in succession until, having been enveloped through one man's treachery, they stood their ground and were hacked to pieces. Moreover, he trains his body, inuring it to labour with all his might, not allowing it to become enervated by baths and ointments and perfumes until it becomes too soft and as unsound as a bad vessel. But some who see him say that he follows these practices out of foolishness and stupidity, having neglected the opportunity to be rich, to be honoured, and to live a life of continual pleasure, and they scorn him, think him insane, and esteem him lightly. Yet he is not enraged at them or vexed; on the contrary, I believe he is kinder to each one than even a father or brothers or friends. And in fact, though he shows respect for his own fellow citizens and friends and kinsmen, still he does not hide his thoughts from them—all the more so because he believes them to be closer to him than all others through home ties and relationship—stressing his words as much as possible and increasing the vehemence of his admonition and exhortation for himself and them alike.

Take, for example, the physician; if he should find it necessary to treat father or mother or his children when they are ill, or even himself through scarcity or lack of other physicians, in case he should need to employ surgery or cautery, he would not, because he loves his children and respects his father and his mother, for that reason cut with a duller knife or cauterize with milder fire, but, on the contrary, he would use the most potent and vigorous treatment possible. For example, they say of Heracles, that when he was unable to heal his body, which had become the victim of a dread malady, he called his sons first of all and ordered them to set fire to him with most brilliant flame; but when they were reluctant and shrank from the ordeal, he abused them as weaklings and unworthy of him and more like their mother, saying, in the words of the poet, "Whither away, ye cravens and disgrace to my engendering, ye likenesses of her, your mother, whom Aetolia bore?" [Euripides, Nauck, *T.G.F.*, adespota 99].

Therefore toward oneself first of all, and also toward one's nearest and dearest, one must behave with fullest frankness and independence, showing no reluctance or yielding in one's words. For far worse than a corrupt and diseased body is a soul which is corrupt, not, I swear, because of slaves or potions or some consuming poison, but rather because of ignorance and depravity and insolence, yes, and jealousy and grief and unnumbered desires. This disease and ailment is more grievous than that of Heracles and requires a far greater and more flaming cautery; and to this healing and release one must summon without demur father or son, kinsman or outsider, citizen or alien.

21 Plutarch elaborates by stressing the need for balance in treating moral illnesses and determining the timeliness of a particular form of frank speech (contrast 2 Tim. 4:2).

Plutarch, *How to Tell a Flatterer from a Friend* **73C–74E**

But since, to quote Euripides, "not everything connected with old age is bad" [*Phoenissae* 528], and the same thing holds true also of our friends' fatuity, we ought to keep close watch upon our friends not only when they go wrong but also when they are right, and indeed the first step should be commendation cheerfully bestowed. Then later, just as steel is made compact by cooling, and takes on a temper as the result of having first been relaxed and softened by heat, so when our friends have become mollified and warmed by our commendations we should give them an application of frankness like a tempering bath. For the right occasion gives us a chance to say, "Is this conduct worthy to compare with that? Do you see what fruits honour yields? This is what we your friends demand; this befits your own character; nature intended you for this." But those other promptings must be exorcised—"Off to the mountain or else the surge of the loud-roaring ocean" [Homer, *Iliad* 6.347]. For as a kind-hearted physician would prefer to relieve a sick man's ailment by sleep and diet rather than by castor and scammony, so a kindly friend, a good father, and a teacher, take pleasure in using commendation rather than blame for the correction of character. For nothing else makes the frank person give so little pain and do so much good by his words, as to refrain from all show of temper, and to approach the erring good-humouredly and with kindliness. For this reason they should not be sharply refuted when they make denial, nor prevented from defending themselves; but we should in some way or other help them to evolve some presentable excuses, and, repudiating the worse motive; provide one more tolerable ourselves, such as is found in Hector's words to his brother: "Strange man! 'Tis not right to nurse this wrath in your bosom" [Homer, *Iliad* 6.326], as though his withdrawal from the combat were not desertion, or cowardice, but only a display of temper. And so Nestor to Agamemnon: "But you to your high-minded spirit gave way" [Homer, *Iliad* 9.109]. For a higher moral tone, I think, is assumed in saying "You acted unbecomingly" rather than "You did wrong," and "You were inadvertent" rather than "You were ignorant," and "Don't be contentious with your brother" rather than "Don't be jealous of your brother," and "Keep away from the woman who is trying to ruin you" rather than "Stop trying to ruin the woman." Such is the method which frankness seeks to take when it would reclaim a wrongdoer; but to stir a man to action it tries the opposite method. For example, whenever it either becomes necessary to divert persons that are on the point of doing wrong, or when we would give an earnest impulse to those who are trying to make a stand against the onset of a violent adverse impulse, or who are quite without energy and spirit for what is noble, we should turn round and ascribe their action to some unnatural or unbecoming motives. Thus Odysseus, as Sophocles represents him, in trying to rouse the spirit of Achilles, says that Achilles is not angry on account of the dinner, but "Already at the sight of builded Troy you are afraid" [Sophocles, *Dinner-guests?*]. And again when Achilles is exceedingly indignant at this, and says that he is for sailing away, Odysseus says, "I know what 'tis you flee; not ill repute, but Hector's near; it is not good to stay" [Sophocles, *Dinner-guests?*]. So by alarming the spirited and manly man with an imputation of cowardice, the chaste and orderly with an imputation of licentiousness, the liberal and lordly with an imputation of pettiness and stinginess, they give to such persons an impulse toward what is noble, and turn them away from what is disgraceful, proving themselves moderate in matters beyond remedy, and owning more to sorrow and sympathy than to blame in their frank speaking; but in efforts to prevent the commission of error and in any wrestling with the emotions they are severe, inexorable, and unremitting. For this is the right time for a resolute goodwill and genuine frankness.

Blame for past deeds is a weapon which we see enemies using against each other. Whereby is confirmed the saying of Diogenes that as a matter of self-preservation, a man needs to be supplied with good friends or else with ardent enemies; for the former instruct him, and the latter take him to task. But it is better to guard against errors by following proffered advice than to repent of errors because of men's upbraiding. This is the reason why it is necessary to treat frankness as a fine art, inasmuch as it is the greatest and most potent medicine in friendship, always needing, however, all care to hit the right occasion, and a tempering with moderation.

Since, then, as has been said, frankness, from its very nature, is oftentimes painful to the person to whom it is applied, there is need to follow the example of the physicians; for they, in surgical operation, do not leave the part that has been operated upon in its suffering and pain, but treat it with soothing lotions and fomentations; nor do persons that use admonition with skill simply apply its bitterness and sting, and then run away; but by further converse and gentle words they mollify and assuage, even as stonecutters smooth and polish the portions of statues that have been previously hammered and chiselled. But the man who has been hard hit and scored by frankness, if he be left rough and tumid and uneven, will, owing to the effect of anger, not readily respond to an appeal the next time, or put up with attempts to soothe him. Therefore those who employ admonition should be particularly on their guard in this respect, and not take their leave too soon, nor allow anything painful and irritating to their acquaintances to form the final topic of conversation at an interview.

THE RESPONSE SOUGHT

Philosophers, in their protreptic speeches (see pp. 122–124), called people to turn to the philosophical life and, having taken that initial step by their own free will (31), to continue living the rational, disciplined life.

22   The conversion of Polemo (fourth century B.C.) to the Academy by Xenocrates, a disciple of Plato, is recounted numberless times in ancient literature to illustrate the deliberate choice that was necessary and the personal transformation that the convert underwent. The setting of this speech is a mock trial in which the Academy, representing philosophy, defends herself against Intemperance's charge that she had robbed Intemperance of her slave Polemo.

Lucian, *The Double Indictment* 17

Heard casually, gentlemen of the jury, the plea which the advocate has made in behalf of Intemperance is quite plausible, but if you give an unprejudiced hearing to my plea also, you will find out that I have done her no wrong at all.

This man Polemo, who, she says, is her servant, was not naturally bad or inclined to Intemperance, but had a nature like mine. But while he was still young and impressionable she preempted him, with the assistance of Pleasure, who usually helps her, and corrupted the poor fellow, surrendering him unconditionally to dissipation and to light women, so that he had not the slightest remnant of shame. In fact, what she thought was said on her behalf a moment ago, you should consider said on my behalf. The poor fellow went about from early to late with garlands on his head, flushed with wine, attended by music right through the public square, never sober, making roisterous calls upon everybody, a disgrace to his ancestors and to the whole city and a laughingstock to strangers.

But when he came to my house, it chanced that, as usual, the doors were wide open and I was discoursing about virtue and temperance to such of my friends as were there. Coming in upon us with his flute and his garlands, first of all he began to shout and tried to break up our meeting by disturbing it with noise. But we paid no attention to him, and as he was not entirely sodden with Intemperance, little by little he grew sober under the influence of our discourses, took off his garlands, silenced his flute-player, became ashamed of his purple mantle, and, awaking, as it were, from profound sleep saw his own condition and condemned his past life. The flush that came from Intemperance faded and vanished, and he flushed for shame at what he was doing. At length he abandoned her then and there, and took up with me, not because I either invited or constrained him, as this person says, but voluntarily, because he believed the conditions here were better.

Please summon him now, that you may see how he has fared at my hands. . . . Taking this man, gentlemen of the jury, when he was in a ridiculous plight, unable either to talk or to stand on account of his potations, I converted him and sobered him and made him from a slave into a well-behaved,

temperate man, very valuable to the Greeks; and he himself
is grateful to me for it, as are also his relatives on his account.

23   Lucian's account of the conversion (possibly his own) brought
about by Nigrinus describes the effect of Nigrinus' protrepsis
(**49**; cf. Acts 2:37–42; 1 Cor. 14:24–25; *2 Clem.* 19; Hermas,
Mand. 3.3; 12.4), the convert's intellectual and emotional at-
tachment to his teacher, and the teacher's continuing role in
his moral development (cf. 1 Cor. 4:14–17; Phil. 2:25–30; 1
Thess. 3:6–10). The account is given in the form of a dialogue
in which one partner (B) recounts his experience as he listened
to the philosopher.

Lucian, *Nigrinus* 3–7, 35–37

3–7. B. "Beginning to talk on these topics and to explain his
position, my dear fellow, [Nigrinus] poured enough ambrosial speech over me to put out of date the famous Sirens
(if there ever were any) and the nightingales and the lotus
of Homer. A divine utterance! For he went on to praise
philosophy and the freedom that it gives, and to ridicule the
things that are popularly considered blessings—wealth and
reputation; dominion and honour, yes and purple and gold
—things accounted very desirable by most men, and till then
by me also. I took it all in with eager, wide-open soul, and
at the moment I couldn't imagine what had come over me;
I was all confused. At first I felt hurt because he had criti-
cised what was dearest in me—wealth and money and reputation,—and I all but cried over their downfall; and then I
thought them paltry and ridiculous, and was glad to be looking up, as it were, out of the murky atmosphere of my past
life to a clear sky and a great light. In consequence, I actually
forgot my eye and its ailment—would you believe it?—and
by degrees grew sharper-sighted in my soul; which, all una-
wares, I had been carrying about in a purblind condition till
then. I went on and on, and so got into the state with which
you just now reproached me: what he said has made me
proud and exalted, and in a word, I take no more notice of
trifles. I suppose I have had the same sort of experience with
philosophy that the Hindoos are said to have had with wine
when they first tasted it. As they are by nature more hot-
blooded than we, on taking such strong drink they became

uproarious at once, and were crazed by the unwatered beverage twice as much as other people. There you have it! I am going about enraptured and drunk with the wine of his discourse."

A. "Why, that isn't drunkenness, it is sobriety and temperance! I should like to hear just what he said, if possible. It is far, very far from right, in my opinion, to be stingy with it, especially if the person who wants to hear is a friend and has the same interests."

B. "Cheer up, good soul! you spur a willing horse, as Homer says, and if you hadn't got ahead of me, I myself should have begged you to listen to my tale, for I want to have you bear witness before the world that my madness has reason in it. Then, too, I take pleasure in calling his words to mind frequently, and have already made it a regular exercise: even if nobody happens to be at hand, I repeat them to myself two or three times a day just the same. I am in the same case with lovers. In the absence of the objects of their fancy they think over their actions and their words, and by dallying with these beguile their lovesickness into the belief that they have their sweethearts near; in fact, sometimes they even imagine they are chatting with them and are as pleased with what they formerly heard as if it were just being said, and by applying their minds to the memory of the past give themselves no time to be annoyed by the present. So I, too, in the absence of my mistress Philosophy, get no little comfort out of gathering together the words that I then heard and turning them over to myself. In short, I fix my gaze on that man as if he were a lighthouse and I were adrift at sea in the dead of night, fancying him by me whenever I do anything and always hearing him repeat his former words. Sometimes, especially when I put pressure on my soul, his face appears to me and the sound of his voice abides in my ears. Truly, as the comedian says, 'he left a sting implanted in his hearers!' " [Eupolis, *Demes* (Kock 94)].

35–37. B. When he had said this and much more of the same sort, he ended his talk. Until then I had listened to him in awe, fearing that he would cease. When he stopped, I felt like the Phaeacians of old, for I stared at him a long time spellbound. Afterwards, in a great fit of confusion and giddiness, I dripped with sweat, I stumbled and stuck in the endeavour to speak, my voice failed, my tongue faltered, and finally I began to cry in embarrassment; for the effect he produced in me was not superficial or casual. My wound was deep and vital, and his words, shot with great accuracy, clove, if I may say so, my very soul in twain. For if I too may now adopt the language of a philosopher, my conception of the matter is that the soul of a well-endowed man resembles a very tender target. Many bowmen, their quivers full of words of all sorts and kinds, shoot at it during life, but not with success in every case. Some draw to the head and let fly harder than they should: though they hit the target, their arrows do not stick in it, but owing to their momentum go through and continue their flight, leaving only a gaping wound in the soul. Others, again, do the opposite; themselves too weak, their bows too slack, the arrows do not even carry to the target as a rule, but often fall spent at half the distance; and if ever they do carry, they strike "with a mere fret o' the skin" and do not make a deep wound, as they were not sped with a strong pull. But a good bowman like Nigrinus first of all scans the target closely for fear that it may be either very soft or too hard for his arrow—for of course there are impenetrable targets. When he is clear on this point, he dips his arrow, not in venom like those of the Scythians nor in vegetable poison like those of the Curetes, but in a sweet, gently-working drug, and then shoots with skill. The arrow, driven by just the right amount of force, penetrates to the point of passing through, and then sticks fast and gives off a quantity of the drug, which naturally spreads and completely pervades the soul. That is why people laugh and cry as they listen, as I did—of course the drug was quietly circulating in my soul. I could not help quoting him the well-known line: "Shoot thus, and bring, mayhap, a ray of hope" [Homer, *Iliad* 8.282]. Not everyone who hears the Phrygian flute goes frantic, but only those who are possessed of Rhea and are put in mind of their condition by the music. In like manner, naturally, not all who listen to philosophers go away enraptured and wounded, but only those who previously had in their nature some secret bond of kinship with philosophy.

ATTITUDES AND PRACTICES TAUGHT

As the philosophers had responsibilities in the process of moral formation, so did the learners, and frequent advice was given on attitudes and practices that would further their moral growth.

24 Plutarch represents the widespread concern that the philosopher's words be listened to with the preparedness to be benefited by them (cf. Luke 8:13; Acts 17:11; 1 Thess. 2:13; James
1:21). He is also careful to warn novices not to be disappointed
by the slowness of the progress they are likely to make (cf. 1
Cor. 3:1-3; 1 Thess. 3:10; Heb. 5:11-14; James 1:22-25), and
to instill responsibility in them for bettering themselves.

Plutarch, *On Listening to Lectures* **46D–47D**

To hear a reprehension or admonition to reform character,
delivered in words that penetrate like a biting drug, and not
to be humbled at hearing it, not to run into a sweating and
dizziness, not to burn with shame in the soul, but, on the
contrary to listen unmoved, grinning, dissembling in the
face of it all, is a notable sign of an illiberal nature in the
young, dead to all modesty because of an habitual and continued acquaintance with wrongdoing, with a soul like hard
and calloused flesh, upon which no lash can leave a weal.

Such is the behaviour of those who belong to this class.
But young men of the opposite temperament, if they ever
hear a single word directed against themselves, run away
without looking back, and try to desert philosophy; and,
although the sense of modesty which Nature has bestowed
upon them is an admirable beginning for their salvation,
they lose it through effeminacy and weakness, since they
display no firmness under reproof, nor do they accept cor-
rections with the proper spirit, but they turn away their ears
toward the agreeable and gentle converse of sundry flatter-
ers or voluble talkers, who enchant them with useless and
unprofitable but nevertheless pleasant utterances. Just as
one who runs away from the physician after an operation,
and will not submit to be bandaged, sustains all the pain of
the treatment, but waits not for its benefits: so when the
word has cut and wounded a man's foolishness, if he gives
it no chance to heal and quiet the wound, he comes away
from philosophy with a smart and pain but with no benefit.
For not only the wound of Telephus, as Euripides says, "is
soothed by fine-rasped filings from the spear" [Nauck,
T.G.F. 724], but the smart from philosophy which sinks deep
in young men of good parts is healed by the very words
which inflicted the hurt. For this reason he who is taken to
task must feel and suffer some smart, yet he should not be

crushed or dispirited, but, as though at a solemn rite of novitiate which consecrates him to philosophy, he should submit to the initial purifications and commotions, in the expectation that something delectable and splendid will follow upon his present distress and perturbation. Indeed, even if the reproof seems to be given unjustly, it is an admirable thing to endure it with continued patience while the man is speaking; and when he has come to the end, to go to him with an explanation, and beg him to reserve for some real misconduct the frankness and earnestness that he has employed in the present instance.

Moreover, just as in learning to read and write, or in taking up music or physical training, the first lessons are attended with much confusion, hard work, and uncertainty, but later, as the learner makes progress, by slow degrees, just as in his relations with human beings, a full familiarity is engendered and knowledge which renders everything attractive, feasible, and easy, both to say and to do, so also is it with philosophy, which undoubtedly has something knotty and unfamiliar in its terms and subject matter at the outset; yet one ought not to take fright at its beginnings, and to abandon it in timorous and craven fashion; rather should he examine each point, and persist and stick to the task of getting on, while awaiting that familiarity which makes every noble thing a pleasure. For come it will without long delay, bringing with it abundant light for the subject of study; it will inspire also a passionate love for virtue; and anyone who could endure to pass the rest of his life without this passion, because he has exiled himself from philosophy for want of true manliness, brands himself either as a very presumptuous man or else a coward.

It is quite possible that the subject of philosophy contains some matter which is difficult for young and inexperienced students to apprehend at the outset. But, at the same time, they must hold themselves responsible for most of the uncertainty and misunderstanding in which they find themselves involved, since quite opposite characters come to fall into the same error. Some, because of a feeling of shame and a desire to spare the speaker, hesitate to ask questions and to get the argument firmly fixed in their minds, nodding their heads in assent as though they comprehended it; others, led by an unreasonable ambition and inane rivalry with their fellow-students, to show off their acuteness and their ability to learn easily, avow that they have the meaning before they have grasped it, and so do not grasp it at all. Then the result is that those modest and silent persons, after leaving the lecture, distress themselves over their difficulties, and finally, driven by necessity, with even greater shame this time, they trouble the lecturers with questions which they should have asked before, and try to catch up; but with the ambitious and self-confident young men, the result is that they are all the time trying to cover up and conceal the ignorance that abides with them.

25   Seneca recognizes that, still pulled in different directions (cf. Rom. 7:15–20), the person who would make moral progress needs helpers, and these, he suggests, can be found in the examples of the ancients who had demonstrated virtue in their deeds (see pp. 135–138; cf. James 2:20–23; 1 Peter 3:5–6). Seneca admired Epicurus, and frequently refers to him when commenting on human nature. For different assessments of the human condition, see pp. 40–47.

Seneca, *Epistle* 52.1–9

Seneca to Lucilius, greeting. What is this force, Lucilius, that drags us in one direction when we are aiming in another, urging us on to the exact place from which we long to withdraw? What is it that wrestles with our spirit, and does not allow us to desire anything once for all? We veer from plan to plan. None of our wishes is free, none is unqualified, none is lasting. "But it is the fool," you say, "who is inconsistent; nothing suits him for long." But how or when can we tear ourselves away from this folly? No man by himself has sufficient strength to rise above it; he needs a helping hand, and some one to extricate him.

Epicurus remarks that certain men have worked their way to the truth without any one's assistance, carving out their own passage. And he gives special praise to these, for their impulse has come from within, and they have forged to the front by themselves. Again, he says, there are others who need outside help, who will not proceed unless someone leads the way, but who will follow faithfully. Of these, he says, Metrodorus was one; this type of man is also excellent, but belongs to the second grade. We ourselves are not of that first class, either; we shall be well treated if we are admitted into the second. Nor need you despise a man who can gain salvation only with the assistance of another; the will to be saved means a great deal, too.

You will find still another class of man,—and a class not to be despised,—who can be forced and driven into righteousness, who do not need a guide as much as they require someone to encourage and, as it were, to force them along. This is the third variety. If you ask me for a man of this pattern also, Epicurus tells us that Hermarchus was such. And of the two last-named classes, he is more ready to congratulate the one, but he feels more respect for the other, for although both reached the same goal, it is a greater credit to have brought about the same result with the more difficult material upon which to work.

Suppose that two buildings have been erected, unlike as to their foundations, but equal in height and in grandeur. One is built on faultless ground, and the process of erection goes right ahead. In the other case, the foundations have exhausted the building materials, for they have been sunk into soft and shifting ground and much labour has been wasted in reaching the solid rock. As one looks at both of them, one sees clearly what progress the former has made, but the larger and more difficult part of the latter is hidden. So with men's dispositions; some are pliable and easy to manage, but others have to be laboriously wrought out by hand, so to speak, and are wholly employed in the making of their own foundations. I should accordingly deem more fortunate the man who has never had any trouble with himself; but the other, I feel, has deserved better of himself, who has won a victory over the meanness of his own nature, and has not gently led himself, but has wrestled his way, to wisdom.

You may be sure that this refractory nature, which demands much toil, has been implanted in us. There are obstacles in our path; so let us fight, and call to our assistance some helpers. "Whom," you say, "shall I call upon? Shall it be this man or that?" There is another choice also open to you; you may go to the ancients; for they have the time to help you. We can get assistance not only from the living, but from those of the past. Let us choose, however, from among the living, not men who pour forth their words with the greatest glibness, turning out commonplaces, and holding, as it were, their own little private exhibitions,—not these, I say, but men who teach us by their lives, men who tell us what we ought to do and then prove it by practice, who show us what we should avoid, and then are never caught doing that which they have ordered us to avoid.

Choose as a guide one whom you will admire more when you see him act than when you hear him speak. Of course I would not prevent you from listening also to those philosophers who are wont to hold public meetings and discussions, provided they appear before the people for the express purpose of improving themselves and others, and do not practise their profession for the sake of self-seeking. For what is baser than philosophy courting applause? Does the sick man praise the surgeon while he is operating?

26 Seneca himself had undergone a transformation (cf. Rom. 12: 2); he is convinced, however, that association with like-minded persons is superior (cf. Col. 3:1–17; 1 Peter 1:22–2:10).

Seneca, *Epistle* 6

Seneca to Lucilius, greeting. I feel, my dear Lucilius, that I am being not only reformed, but transformed. I do not yet, however, assure myself, or indulge the hope, that there are no elements left in me which need to be changed. Of course there are many that should be made more compact, or made thinner, or be brought into greater prominence. And indeed this very fact is proof that my spirit is altered into something better,—that it can see its own faults, of which it was previously ignorant. In certain cases sick men are congratulated because they themselves have perceived that they are sick.

I therefore wish to impart to you this sudden change in myself; I should then begin to place a surer trust in our friendship,—the true friendship, which hope and fear and self-interest cannot sever, the friendship in which and for the sake of which men meet death. I can show you many who have lacked, not a friend, but a friendship; this, however, cannot possibly happen when souls are drawn together by identical inclinations into an alliance of honourable desires. And why can it not happen? Because in such cases men know that they have all things in common, especially their troubles.

You cannot conceive what distinct progress I notice that each day brings to me. And when you say, "Give me also a share in these gifts which you have found so helpful," I reply that I am anxious to heap all these privileges upon you, and that I am glad to learn in order that I may teach. Nothing will ever please me, no matter how excellent or beneficial, if I must retain the knowledge of it to myself. And if wisdom were given me under the express condition that it must be kept hidden and not uttered, I should refuse it. No good thing is pleasant to possess, without friends to share it.

I shall therefore send to you the actual books; and in order that you may not waste time in searching here and there for profitable topics, I shall mark certain passages, so that you can turn at once to those which I approve and admire. Of course, however, the living voice and the intimacy of a common life will help you more than the written word. You must go to the scene of action, first, because men put more faith in their eyes than in their ears, and second, because the way is long if one follows patterns. Cleanthes could not have been the express image of Zeno, if he had merely heard his lectures; he shared in his life, saw into his hidden purposes, and watched him to see whether he lived according to his own rules. Plato, Aristotle, and the whole throng of sages who were destined to go each his different way, derived more benefit from the character than from the words of Socrates. It was not the class-room of Epicurus, but living together under the same roof, that made great men of Metrodorus, Hermarchus, and Polyaenus. Therefore I summon you, not merely that you may derive benefit, but that you may confer benefit; for we can assist each other greatly.

Meanwhile, I owe you my little daily contribution; you shall be told what pleased me today in the writings of Hecato; it is these words: "What progress, you ask, have I made? I have begun to be a friend to myself." That was indeed a great benefit; such a person can never be alone. You may be sure that such a man is a friend to all mankind. Farewell.

27 Seneca recommends philosophical study out of the conviction that his predecessors had toiled for his benefit (cf. Rom. 4:23; 15:4; 1 Cor. 9:9–10; 10:10–11), but urges that traditional wisdom or paraenesis (see pp. 124–129) be adapted to particular circumstances (cf. 1 Cor. 7:10–11, 17). The traditional nature of paraenesis has led some scholars to question whether paraenesis had any direct relation to the situation to which it was addressed. This passage shows that the more reflective philosophers were acutely aware of the need to adapt their teaching.

Seneca, *Epistle* 64.6–10

And virtue herself will have the same effect upon you, of making you admire her and yet hope to attain her. In my own case, at any rate, the very contemplation of wisdom takes much of my time; I gaze upon her with bewilderment, just as I sometimes gaze upon the firmament itself, which I often behold as if I saw it for the first time. Hence I worship the discoveries of wisdom and their discoverers; to enter, as it were, into the inheritance of many predecessors is a delight. It was for me that they laid up this treasure; it was for me that they toiled. But we should play the part of a careful householder; we should increase what we have inherited. This inheritance shall pass from me to my descendants larger than before. Much still remains to do, and much will always remain, and he who shall be born a thousand ages hence will not be barred from his opportunity of adding something further. But even if the old masters have discovered everything, one thing will be always new,—the application and the scientific study and classification of the discoveries made by others. Assume that prescriptions have been handed down to us for the healing of the eyes; there is no need of my searching for others in addition; but for all that, these prescriptions must be adapted to the particular disease and to the particular stage of the disease. Use this prescription to relieve granulation of the eyelids, that to reduce the swelling of the lids, this to prevent sudden pain or a rush of tears, that to sharpen the vision. Then compound these several prescriptions, watch for the right time of their application, and apply the proper treatment in each case.

The cures for the spirit also have been discovered by the ancients; but it is our task to learn the method and the time of treatment. Our predecessors have worked much improvement, but have not worked out the problem. They deserve respect, however, and should be worshipped with a divine ritual. Why should I not keep statues of great men to kindle my enthusiasm, and celebrate their birthdays? Why should I not continually greet them with respect and honour? The reverence which I owe to my own teachers I owe in like measure to those teachers of the human race, the source from which the beginnings of such great blessings have flowed. If I meet a consul or a praetor, I shall pay him all the honour which his post of honour is wont to receive: I shall dismount, uncover, and yield the road. What, then? Shall I admit into my soul with less than the highest marks of respect Marcus Cato, the Elder and the Younger, Laelius the Wise, Socrates and Plato, Zeno and Cleanthes? I worship them in very truth, and always rise to do honour to such noble names.

28 Epictetus envisages a regimen to be followed, beginning when the learner arises in the morning and extending through all his daily activities.

Epictetus, *Discourse* 1.4.18–21

Where, then, is progress? If any man among you, withdrawing from eternal things, has turned his attention to the question of his own moral purpose, cultivating and perfecting it so as to make it finally harmonious with nature, elevated, free, unhindered, untrammelled, faithful, and honourable; and if he has learned that he who craves or shuns the things that are not under his control can be neither faithful nor free, but must himself of necessity be changed and tossed to and fro with them, and must end by subordinating himself to others, those, namely, who are able to procure or prevent these things that he craves or shuns, and if, finally, when he rises in the morning he proceeds to keep and observe all this that he has learned; if he bathes as a faithful man, eats as a self-respecting man,—similarly, whatever the subject matter may be with which he has to deal, putting into practice his guiding principles, as the runner does when he applies the principles of running, and the voice-trainer when he applies the principles of voice-training,—this is the man who in all truth is making progress, and the man who has not travelled at random is this one.

4

Means of Instruction

Moral instruction was given through a variety of means, some of which are here offered by way of illustration. In addition to these, among the most common, on a learned level, were treatises or essays (**71**; cf. Hermas, *Mandates*) which were frequently delivered as lectures before they were circulated in written form (e.g., **53, 67**).

SPEECHES

The preferred way of instructing was through speech. Writers like Seneca (**17**) regarded letters as the next best. Philosophers liked to emphasize that they were different from orators, whom they accused of playing to their audiences, yet even in their letters they frequently commented on the appropriate rhetorical style of the philosopher and criticized those whose eloquence had become an end in itself (**1**; cf. 1 Cor. 2:1–5). With a possible few exceptions (e.g., Hebrews; 1 John; *2 Clement*), the early Christian writings that have been preserved were not originally speeches. Nevertheless, that they were dictated (cf. Rom. 16:22) and intended to be read aloud to congregations (cf. 1 Thess. 5:27; Rev. 1:3), thus functioning like speeches or sermons, meant that the writers were conscious of oral style.

29   Seneca begins this letter by complimenting his correspondent on fulfilling the requirement of epistolographic theoreticians (see pp. 79–82) that a letter accurately reflect its writer's personality (contrast 2 Cor. 10:10), and then comments on the philosopher's speech. His chief requirements are that the philosopher's speech reflect his own composed, dignified character, be measured in pace, and be capable of effecting change in his hearers (cf. James 3:1–12).

Seneca, *Epistle* 40.1–8, 13–14

1–8. Seneca to Lucilius, greeting. I thank you for writing to me so often; for you are revealing your real self to me in the only way you can. I never receive a letter from you without being in your company forthwith. If the pictures of our absent friends are pleasing to us, though they only refresh the memory and lighten our longing by a solace that is unreal and unsubstantial, how much more pleasant is a letter, which brings us real traces, real evidences, of an absent friend! For that which is sweetest when we meet face to face is afforded by the impress of a friend's hand upon his letter,—recognition.

You write me that you heard a lecture by the philosopher Serapio, when he landed at your present place of residence. "He is wont," you say, "to wrench up his words with a mighty rush, and he does not let them flow forth one by one, but makes them crowd and dash upon each other. For the words come in such quantity that a single voice is inadequate to utter them." I do not approve of this in a philosopher; his speech, like his life, should be composed; and nothing that rushes headlong and is hurried is well ordered. That is why, in Homer, the rapid style, which sweeps down without a break like a snow-squall, is assigned to the younger speaker; from the old man eloquence flows gently, sweeter than honey.

Therefore, mark my words; that forceful manner of speech, rapid and copious, is more suited to a mountebank than to a man who is discussing and teaching an important and serious subject. But I object just as strongly that he should drip out his words as that he should go at top speed; he should neither keep the ear on the stretch, nor deafen it. For that poverty-stricken and thin-spun style also makes the audience less attentive because they are weary of its stammering slowness; nevertheless, the word which has been long awaited sinks in more easily than the word which flits past us on the wing. Finally, people speak of "handing down" precepts to their pupils; but one is not "handing down" that which eludes the grasp. Besides, speech that

deals with the truth should be unadorned and plain. This
popular style has nothing to do with the truth; its aim is to
impress the common herd, to ravish heedless ears by its
speed; it does not offer itself for discussion, but snatches
itself away from discussion. But how can that speech govern
others which cannot itself be governed? May I not also remark that all speech which is employed for the purpose of
healing our minds, ought to sink into us? Remedies do not
avail unless they remain in the system.

Besides, this sort of speech contains a great deal of sheer
emptiness; it has more sound than power. My terrors should
be quieted, my irritations soothed, my illusions shaken off,
my indulgences checked, my greed rebuked. And which of
these cures can be brought about in a hurry? What physician
can heal his patient on a flying visit? May I add that such
jargon of confused and ill-chosen words cannot afford pleasure, either? No; but just as you are well satisfied, in the
majority of cases, to have seen through tricks which you did
not think could possibly be done, so in the case of these
word-gymnasts,—to have heard them once is amply sufficient. For what can a man desire to learn or to imitate in
them? What is he to think of their souls, when their speech
is sent into the charge in utter disorder, and cannot be kept
in hand? Just as, when you run down hill, you cannot stop
at the point where you had decided to stop, but your steps
are carried along by the momentum of your body and are
borne beyond the place where you wished to halt; so this
speech has no control over itself, nor is it seemly for philosophy; since philosophy should carefully place her words, not
fling them out, and should proceed step by step.

"What then?" you say; "should not philosophy sometimes
take a loftier tone?" Of course she should; but dignity of
character should be preserved, and this is stripped away by
such violent and excessive force. Let philosophy possess
great forces, but kept well under control; let her stream flow
unceasingly, but never become a torrent. And I should
hardly allow even to an orator a rapidity of speech like this,
which cannot be called back, which goes lawlessly ahead; for
how could it be followed by jurors, who are often inexperienced and untrained? Even when the orator is carried
away by his desire to show off his powers, or by uncontrolla-
ble emotion, even then he should not quicken his pace and
heap up words to an extent greater than the ear can endure.

13–14. However, I have this further reason for frightening you away from the latter malady, namely, that you could only be successful in practising this style by losing your sense of modesty; you would have to rub all shame from your countenance, and refuse to hear yourself speak. For that heedless flow will carry with it many expressions which you would wish to criticize. And, I repeat, you could not attain it and at the same time preserve your sense of shame. Moreover, you would need to practise every day, and transfer your attention from subject matter to words. But words, even if they came to you readily and flowed without any exertion on your part, yet would have to be kept under control. For just as a less ostentatious gait becomes a philosopher, so does a restrained style of speech, far removed from boldness. Therefore, the ultimate kernel of my remarks is this: I bid you be slow of speech. Farewell.

30 Plutarch explains, in psychological terms, why, from the listener's side, speech is the most powerful means. Beginning with a statement by Theophrastus, who succeeded Aristotle as head of the Peripatetic school around 323 B.C., he claims that hearing is more rational than emotional, yet of all the senses is most capable of causing the type of emotional response that the philosopher aims at in his protrepsis (**22–24**). Great care should therefore be exercised in speaking (cf. Eph. 5:3–4; Col. 4:6; 1 Tim. 4:13–16), for as the living voice can contribute to one's growth toward virtue, it can also pervert, especially the young, to vice. Ever mindful of the discrimination that should be exercised in the therapy of the word (**21**), he differs radically from the unforgiving, brutal laceration of the rigorous Cynic (**18**; cf. 2 Tim. 2:24–25).

Plutarch, *On Listening to Lectures* 37F–38D

I think you may not find unwelcome some preliminary remarks about the sense of hearing, which Theophrastus asserts is the most emotional of all the senses. For nothing which can be seen or tasted or touched brings on such distractions, confusions, and excitements, as take possession of the soul when certain crashing, clashing, and roaring noises assail the hearing. Yet this sense is more rational than emotional. For while many places and parts of the body make way for vice to enter through them and fasten itself upon the

soul, virtue's only hold upon the young is afforded by the
ears, if they be uncontaminated and kept from the outset
unspoiled by flattery and untouched by vile words. For this
reason Xenocrates advised putting ear-protectors on children rather than on athletes, on the ground that the latter
have only their ears disfigured by the blows they receive,
while the former have their characters disfigured by the
words they hear; not that he would thus court heedlessness
or deafness, but he advises vigilance against vile words, until
such time as other words, of good sort, fostered in the character by philosophy, should, like watchmen, have taken
under their charge the post chiefly exposed to influence and
persuasion. And Bias of old [one of the Seven Wise Men of
Greece, sixth century B.C.], on receiving orders to send to
Amasis [king of Egypt] the portion of the sacrificial animal
which was at the same time the best and the worst, cut out
the tongue and sent it to him, on the ground that speech
contains both injuries and benefits in the largest measure.
Most people in bestowing an affectionate kiss on little children not only take hold of the children by the ears but bid
the children to do the same by them, thus insinuating in a
playful way that they must love most those who confer benefit through the ears. For surely the fact is plain, that the
young man who is debarred from hearing all instruction and
gets no taste of speech not only remains wholly unfruitful
and makes no growth towards virtue, but may also be perverted towards vice, and the product of his mind, like that
of a fallow and untilled piece of ground, will be a plentiful
crop of wild oats. For if the impulses towards pleasure and
the feelings of suspicion towards hard work (which are not
of external origin nor imported products of the spoken
word, but indigenous sources, as it were, of pestilent emotions and disorders without number) be allowed to continue
unconstrained along their natural channels, and if they be
not either removed or diverted another way through the
agency of goodly discourse, thus putting the natural endow-
ments in a fit condition, there is not one of the wild beasts
but would be found more civilized than man.

31 This oration of Maximus illustrates how a moralist of moderate
mien used various devices in protreptic speech. It is included
in its entirety for that reason and as an example of a speech by

a professional rhetorician. Maximus begins by telling, in the
manner of Aesop, the famous creator of animal fables, a fable
describing the Golden Age, that imaginary early age in which
humanity was ideally happy, prosperous, and innocent (1), and
then depicts the degeneration of the race (2). With these types
of lives characterized and opposed, he calls for voluntary
change in his listeners (3). Using lists of vices (4c; see pp.
138–141), he further portrays lives of vice and virtue, compar-
ing the former to prison (4a–d), the latter to freedom (4e–f),
and rhetorically asks which should be chosen (4gh). Diogenes
is then offered as an example of the ideal life (5; cf. pp. 135–
140). The depiction of Diogenes, given in antithetic form ("not
. . . but"), refers to the advice he received from Apollo, but
stresses that he liberated himself from his bonds and the common hardships of life (5b; cf. pp. 141–143), describes his independent manner of life (5c–f), and characterizes his admonition as placing a premium on his deeds over his words (5g; cf.
pp. 38–40). This, Maximus concludes, returning to the issues
of free will and hardships, is the life to be preferred (6). In this
speech, Maximus uses Stoic and Cynic traditions. The former
is evident in his reference to the divine, which reflects Stoic
concern to harmonize their views of providence and free will.
Maximus, however, is no profound thinker and does not here
pursue that concern. Furthermore, the oration has the practical aim of converting his audience to a particular mode of life.
Therefore he offers a picture of Diogenes the Cynic that lays
stress on his free choice.

Maximus of Tyre, *Discourse* **36 (***Maximi Tyrii philosophoumena,***
ed. H. Hobein [Leipzig: Teubner, 1910], 412–425). The
translation consists of the sections printed in Arthur O.
Lovejoy and George Boas,** *Primitivism and Related Ideas in
Antiquity* **(Baltimore: Johns Hopkins University Press, 1935),
148–151, supplemented by my own.**

(1a) I wish to compose for you a fable conforming to the
Lydian's art. The speakers in it, however, will not be a lion,
nor an eagle, nor things still less vocal than these, namely
oaks, but will be as follows: (b) Zeus existed, and heaven and
earth, and in heaven its citizens, the gods; but men, the
nurselings of earth, had not yet seen the light of day. (c) Zeus
therefore called Prometheus and bade him settle upon the
earth an animal which should be simple, in mind approach-

ing very near to the gods, in body slender, erect and sym-
metrical, mild of aspect, ready to work with his hands, and
firm of step. (d) Prometheus obeyed the command of Zeus,
and made men and settled the earth with them. (e) And after
they had been created, they lived without difficulty. For the
earth provided them with food in abundance, grassy mead-
ows and leafy mountains and plentiful fruits, such as it usually bears when it is undisturbed by farmers. The nymphs
also supplied them with pure fountains, clear rivers, and
abundant, easily accessible sources of other streams. (f) In
addition, the sun's warmth made their bodies comfortable
by surrounding them in the right measure, and in summer
cooling breezes from the rivers refreshed their bodies. (g)
Among men thus enjoying an unlimited wealth of goods
freely furnished them, strife was unknown. (h) The poets
seem to me to have come very close to this myth of ours
when, speaking in parables, they describe a life of this kind
under Saturn, king of the gods; a life without war, without
weapons, without guards, quiet, peaceful, healthful, free
from poverty. And it was this, it seems, that Hesiod, speaking of it in a boastful way in comparison with us, called the
Golden Race.

(2a) But here I leave the fable. Let us turn to the argument
which arises from it, and proceed to compare one manner
of life with another, the earlier with the later, whether this
be called "iron" or by some other name. When, then, men
had the earth allotted to them, they divided it up in portions
amongst themselves, surrounded themselves with fortifications, and wrapped soft cloths about their bodies and protected their feet with skins; and some hung gold about their
necks, others about their heads, others about their fingers,
as a kind of charm, both for luck and for ornament; and they
built themselves houses, and invented locks and halls and
gateways. (b) They began, also, to molest the earth by digging and burrowing in it for metals; nor did they leave the
sea unvexed, but constructed on it ships for war and travel
and trade. (c) Even the air they could not let alone, but
plundered it by catching birds with bird-lime and nets and
all manner of devices. (d) They abstained neither from tame
animals on account of their weakness, nor from wild ones
because they were dangerous, but filled their bellies through
slaughter and bloodshed and rapine of every sort. And always they sought for new kinds of enjoyment, disdaining

those to which they were accustomed. (e) By thus pursuing pleasure, they fell into misery. When they sought after wealth, they always considered what they already possessed as mere poverty in comparison with what they lacked, and their acquisitions always fell short of their ambitions. Dreading poverty, they were incapable of being content with sufficiency; (f) fearing death, they took no care of life; seeking to avoid disease, they never abstained from the things that cause it. (g) Full of mutual suspicions, they plotted against most of their fellows. They were cruel to the unarmed and craven towards the armed. (h) They hated tyranny and themselves desired to tyrannize; they blamed base actions but did not refrain from them. (i) Good fortune they admired but not virtue; misfortune they pitied but knavery they did not avoid. When luck was with them they were bold, when it turned against them they were in despair. (k) They declared that the dead are happy, yet themselves clung to life; and on the other hand they hated life, yet were afraid to die. (l) They denounced wars and were incapable of living in peace. In slavery they were abject, in freedom insolent. Under democracy they were turbulent, under tyranny, timid. They desired children, but neglected them when they had them. They prayed to the gods, as to beings able to assist them, they scorned them, as unable to punish; or again, they feared them as avenging powers, and swore falsely, as if the gods had no existence.

(3a) Such, then, being the discord and dissension characteristic of this second kind of life, to which of the two shall we give the prize of victory? Which of them shall we say is the simple life, exempt from difficulties, and of ample liberty, and which the life that is not simple, but constrained, pitiable, full of difficulties? (b) Let a representative of each of them come forward, so that the question may be put to the judgment. Let both be interrogated—first the man who lived the first kind of life, naked, without a house, without arts, who has the whole earth for his city and household. Let us put before him the contrast between his own and the other manner of existence, and ask him whether he prefers to continue in his former way of living and in liberty, or to gain the pleasures of the second sort of life at the cost of the evils which accompany them. (c) After him, let the other present himself, and let the judge put before him, in contrast, the mode of life and the liberty of the former, and then

ask him whether he prefers to remain as he is, or to change
over to that peaceful and unrestrained life, exempt from fear
and from suffering. (d) Which of these men is the one who
will prove the deserter? Which will leave his dwelling-place?
Which will voluntarily exchange one mode of life for the
other?

(4a) Who is so stupid and insensible and wretched that,
through love of small and ephemeral pleasures, dubious
goods, uncertain hopes, and equivocal successes, he will not
remove and migrate to what is admittedly a state of happiness; especially since he knows that he will by this means be
freed from a multitude of evils which are involved in the
second kind of life, and knows, too, how troubled and
wretched and hapless existence is made by them? (b) To
describe each of these lives by a simile: that "noble" and
variegated kind is like a dreadful prison in which unhappy
men, confined in a dark cell, with great irons on their feet,
heavy weights about their necks, and grievous fetters on
their hands, pass their days in filth, in torment, in weeping
and groaning. (c) Nevertheless, through time and custom
they devise for themselves, even in their prison, certain
means of relief and enjoyment—sometimes by getting
drunk, sometimes by all singing at once, sometimes by gour-
mandizing, sometimes by sexual indulgence. Yet fear and
distrust and the recollection of the evils that are present to
them prevent them from ever being quietly satisfied with
these things; (d) so that you may hear in the prison at one
and the same time groans and songs of triumph, lamentation
and rejoicing. (e) But the other sort of life I will liken to that
of a man living in the clear light of day, whose hands and feet
are free, who can turn his neck in any direction, can lift his
eyes to the rising sun, look at the stars, distinguish night
from day, look forward to the changes of the seasons, feel
the winds, and breathe the pure, free air. (f) On the other
hand, he is deprived of the pleasures which accompanied his
confinement in the prison; so that he neither becomes intox-
icated, nor is given to sexual indulgence, nor overeats, nor
groans, nor sings songs of triumph, nor laments, nor is
satiated, but finds sufficient sustenance in a spare and
meagre diet. Which of these shall we consider the image of
happiness? Which sort of life shall we pity? Which shall we
choose? Shall it be life in the prison, mixed and obscure as
it is, ensnared in bitter and pitiful pleasures: "Where joyful

shouts and groans promiscuous rise" [Homer, *Iliad* 4.45], from men who rejoice and weep at the same time? Let not such be *your* choice, O fearful soul!

(5a) Let us, however, leave both similes and myths, and turn to the man who, though he lived, not in the reign of Saturn, but in the midst of this iron race, was nevertheless set free by Zeus and Apollo. (b) This man was neither Attic nor Dorian, he was neither reared by Solon [Athenian lawgiver, sixth century B.C.] nor taught by Lycurgus [Spartan lawgiver], for the virtues do not depend upon the suffrages of places or of laws, but was a native of Sinope in Pontus. After he had taken counsel of Apollo, he divested himself of all unfavorable circumstances, freed himself from bonds and moved about the earth without ties, like a bird endowed with reason—fearing no tyrant, constrained by no law, occupied with no state's business, unencumbered by the care of children, unhampered by marriage, neither fastened to a farm nor burdened with military affairs nor driven from one place to another by trade. (c) Rather, he laughed at all such men and at their pursuits, as we laugh at little children when we see them quarreling over their playthings, beating one another and being beaten, plundering and being plundered.

Indeed, he lived the life of a fearless and free king, not passing the winter in Babylon, nor tiring himself in summer among the Medes, but with the seasons migrated from Attica to the Isthmus, and from the Isthmus to Attica. (d) His palaces were temples and gymnasia and sacred groves. (e) His wealth was the most abundant, the most secure and not exposed to plots, for it consisted of the entire earth and its fruits, together with springs, the offspring of the earth, more copious than all the wine of Lesbos and Chios. He was also a friend, and, accustomed to the air like lions, did not desert the seasons of Zeus, nor contrive against him by fabricating heat during winter and desiring to be cool in summer. (f) He was so adjusted to the nature of the universe that from his manner of life he became healthy and strong, and lived to a ripe old age, having no need of medicine, nor of the knife, nor of fire, nor of Chiron, nor of Asclepius or his descendants, nor of the oracles of soothsayers, the lustrations of priests or the incantations of sorcerers. (g) And when Greece was at war, and everyone was attacking someone else, "Each against each then strove in dreadful fight" [Homer, *Iliad* 3.132], he alone maintained an armistice, moving unarmed among the armed and at peace with all the combatants. The unjust, tyrants, and sycophants kept their hands off him. For he reproved evil men, yet not with sophistries of words, which are the most annoying form of reproof, but on every occasion by his deeds, which are the most efficacious and irenic form of reproof. It was for this reason that no Melitus, nor Aristophanes, nor Lycon rose against Diogenes.

(6a) How is it possible, then, that such a life as this should not have been preferred by Diogenes, which he voluntarily chose, which Apollo had given him and Zeus praised, which people of intellect admire? Or do we think that an unfavorable circumstance is something other than the use of an action which is not voluntarily chosen by the person holding on? (b) Ask a married man, "What is your reason for marrying?" He will answer, "To have children." Ask the man who rears children for what reason he fathered them, and he will answer, for the sake of succession. Ask the soldier why he fights, and he will answer, for gain; the farmer, and he will answer, for produce; the businessman, and he will answer, for wealth; the politician, and he will answer, for honor. (c) But most of these loves miscarry and turn out to the contrary; and success is a matter of prayer, not of judgment or skill.

(d) Everyone who chooses these things passes through life involved in a certain unfavorable circumstance, and endures misery which is not voluntary and which does not come about because of ignorance of self-elected goods. (e) Which of these persons will anyone call free? The demagogue? You are speaking of a slave of many despots. The orator? You are speaking of a slave of vindictive judges. The tyrant? You are speaking of a slave of unbridled pleasures. The general? You are speaking of a slave of uncertain fortune. The sailor? You are speaking of a slave of an unstable art. The philosopher? (f) About which one are you speaking? I do indeed praise Socrates, but I hear him saying, "I obey the law, I willingly go to prison, and willingly take the poison." (g) O Socrates, do you see what you are saying? Do you do so willingly, or do you in a becoming manner set yourself against involuntary fortune? "I obey the law." Which one? For if that of Zeus, I praise the lawgiver, but if that of Solon, in what was Solon superior to Socrates? Let Plato also answer me on behalf of philosophy, if no one has disturbed it—neither

Dion in exile, nor Dionysius [tyrant of Syracuse, fifth to fourth century B.C.] with his threats, nor the Sicilian and Ionian Seas, up and down which he was compelled to sail. (h) And, if I pass on to Xenophon [disciple of Socrates, fifth to fourth century B.C.], I see also his life full of wandering, ambiguous fortune, compulsory military expeditions, involuntary military command, and dignified exile.

(i) I say, therefore, that these unfavorable circumstances are avoided by that life by which Diogenes was more elevated than Lycurgus, Solon, Artaxerxes and Alexander, and freer than Socrates himself, since he was neither led to court nor kept in prison nor praised in consequence of misfortunes.

LETTERS

As early as the fourth century B.C., Epicurus used letters to instruct and direct the affairs of the philosophic communities who held him in esteem as their master. The voluminous correspondence of Cicero and Seneca witness to the popularity of the genre in the centuries immediately before and after Christ. Letters were used in many areas of life and for many purposes. Of particular interest is the way in which letters were used in philosophical propaganda and moral instruction. The letters of Seneca, some of Cicero's, and many of the pseudepigraphic ones, that is, those written in someone else's name (e.g., those attributed to Melissa and Theano), are edifying in a moral sense, while many other pseudepigraphic ones (e.g., those attributed to Crates and Diogenes) advance certain philosophical viewpoints in competition with others.

Some of the pseudepigraphic letters may have been composed as exercises in style. Certain rhetorical theorists gave attention to letter writing and, with astonishing acuteness, classified letters into different types of style. They regarded a letter as one half of a dialogue or a surrogate for an actual dialogue, held a letter to be a speech in the written medium, and insisted that a letter reflect the personality of its writer (contrast 2 Cor. 10:10). Seneca's letters (**17, 29**) demonstrate that, while the philosophers' interests in their letters may have been moral, they were self-conscious about what style was appropriate to the medium they used.

Christian literature of the period under consideration in this book predominantly consists of letters. Some of these, particularly the letters of Paul, are real letters, written to specific situations, but some have artificially been made to look like letters. The letter of

James, for example, is a paraenetic work which has an epistolary opening (James 1:1) but not closing, as one would expect in a real letter (cf. Phil. 4:21–23). For the most part, early Christian letters are of a mixed type, but some represent one style. Thus 1 Thessalonians is a paraenetic letter which Paul has put to a pastoral use, Philemon is a letter of recommendation, as is 3 John (cf. Rom. 16:1–2), and *1 Clement* is a letter of advice.

32   The close relationship of letters to oral communication, plus the examples from the stylistic handbook of Pseudo-Demetrius **(32),** helps us to understand the popularity of letters among moralists who regarded the spoken word as of major importance. The styles of a letter could be mixed, combining, for example, admonition and threat (cf. 1 Cor. 4:14–21).

Pseudo-Demetrius, *Epistolary Types,* **Introduction, Nos. 5–8** (*Demetrii et Libanii qui feruntur Typoi Epistolikoi et Epistolimaioi Charakteres,* **ed. Valentin Weichert [Leipzig: Teubner, 1910])**

Introduction. There are, then, twenty one letter styles that we have come across. Perhaps time, since it is a highly gifted inventor of skills and theories, might produce more than these. But as far as we are concerned, there is no other type that properly pertains to the epistolary mode. Each of them is named after the form of style to which it belongs, as follows: friendly, commendatory, blaming, reproachful, consoling, censorious, admonishing, threatening, vituperative, praising, advisory, supplicatory, inquiring, responding, allegorical, accounting, accusing, apologetic, congratulatory, ironic, thankful.

The consoling type is that written to people who are grieving because something unpleasant has happened to them. It is as follows:

When I heard of the terrible things that you met at the hands of thankless Fate, I felt the deepest grief, considering that what had happened had not happened to you more than to me. When I saw all the things that assailed life, all that day long I cried over them. But then I considered that such things are the common lot of all, with nature establishing neither a particular time or age in which one must suffer anything, but often confronting us secretly, awkwardly and

undeservedly. Since I did not happen to be present to comfort you, I decided to do so by letter. Bear, then, what has
happened as lightly as you can, and exhort yourself just as
you would exhort someone else. For you know that reason
will make it easier for you to be relieved of your grief with
the passage of time.

The censorious type is that written with rebukes on account of errors that have already been made. In the following manner:

Some sins are committed voluntarily and some involun-
tarily, some are major and some minor, some are harmful
only to those who commit them, while others are harmful to
other people as well. But, your sins were like a way of life
with you, for indeed you did not unwillingly commit sins that
are great and harmful to many. It is therefore fitting that
you meet with a more severe rebuke, if indeed in the present
case it has happened that others also have been wronged.
Nevertheless, the trespass that has occurred can still be
remedied. For if you aim to correct your behavior, you yourself will be responsible for its not happening again as it did
before.

The admonishing type is one which indicates through its
name what its character is. For admonition is the instilling
of sense in the person who is being admonished, and teaching him what should and should not be done. In the following manner:

You acted badly when you ill-treated a man who had conducted himself well and had lived according to reason, and
who had, generally speaking, done you no harm. Indeed, if
you had suffered at the hands of someone else, you would
certainly be justified in expecting an apology from him. Re-
alize, therefore, that this action deserves an apology from
you. Do not, then, think that the person who would rebuke
sins has neither parents nor a proper upbringing, nor, worst
of all, that he has no relative or friend.

It is the threatening type when with intensity we instill fear
in people for what they had done or will do. In the following
manner:

If you think that you will not have to give any account for
what you are about to do, then go ahead and do it. But you
will see clearly that neither by soaring to the heights nor
plunging to the depths will you in any manner cause a delay

[in your punishment]. For you would find no way by which to escape what you must suffer.

33 Of the types described by Demetrius, letters of consolation were widely used. Consolation was regarded by rhetoricians and practiced by moralists as belonging to paraenesis (**51 end**; cf. 1 Thess. 4:13–18). It was offered not only at death but on the occasion of all misfortunes that caused grief. This papyrus letter from Oxyrhynchus in Egypt dates from the second century A.D. In it a certain Irene expresses her sympathy to her friends upon having learned of the death of their son. The advice to comfort one another is frequently compared with 1 Thessalonians 4:18.

Papyrus Oxyrhynchus 115. Irene to Taonnophiris and Philo.

Be of good courage! I sorrowed and wept over the departed one as I did over Didymas. I did everything that was fitting, and so did all of my household, Epaphroditus and Thermythion and Philion and Apollonius and Plantas. But, nevertheless, against such things one can do nothing. Therefore comfort one another. Farewell.

PYTHAGOREAN LETTERS

The Pythagorean letters are philosophically eclectic, containing an especially large admixture of Stoicism and Cynicism (**34**). Pythagoreans had a reputation for stressing the importance to society of proper behavior of family members, particularly women and children (see the Augustan historian, Pompeius Trogus, *Historiae Philippicae* 20.4, and cf. 1 Tim. 3:4–5, 11–12; 5:3–16; Titus 2:1–10). Thus, while such advice as is given in the following letters is not uniquely Pythagorean (**36f, 36g, 38**; cf. 1 Peter 3:1–6), it does represent what was thought to be characteristic of them. The prominence given to women in Pythagorean communities is reflected in the writings, in this case letters **34, 35,** attributed to them. The general themes of the letters are that women should be chaste and modest (cf. 1 Tim. 2:9; Titus 2:4–5; 1 Peter 3:3–4; *1 Clem.* 1.3; 21.7; Polycarp, *Phil.* 4.2) and tend to the rearing of their children (**4;** cf. 1 Tim. 5:10; *1 Clem.* 21.8; Polycarp, *Phil.* 4.2; *Did.* 4.9; *Barn.* 19.8)

34

Pseudo-Melissa, *Letter to Kleareta* (Alfons Städele, *Die Briefe des Pythagoras und der Pythagoreer* [Meisenheim: Anton Hain, 1980], 160–162)

It appears to me that on your own accord you have acquired considerable noble qualities. For that you eagerly wish to hear what adorns a woman justifies the hope that you will grow old in virtue. The temperate, freeborn woman must live with her legal husband adorned with modesty, clad in neat, simple, white dress without extravagance or excess. She must avoid clothing that is either entirely purple or is streaked with purple and gold, for that kind of dress is worn by hetaerae when they stalk the masses of men. But the adornment of a woman who wishes to please only one man, her own husband, is her character and not her clothing. For the freeborn woman must be beautiful to her own husband, not to the men in the neighborhood.

You should have a blush on your cheeks as a sign of modesty instead of rouge, and should wear nobility, decorum and temperance instead of gold and emeralds. For the woman who strives for virtue must not have her heart set on expensive clothing but on the management of her household. She must please her husband by doing what he wishes, for a husband's wishes ought to be an unwritten law to an orderly wife, and she should live by them. She should be of the opinion that, together with herself, she brought to him her orderly behavior as the most beautiful and greatest dowry. For she must trust more in the beauty and riches of her soul than of her face or money. For the former can strip away envy and illness, but the latter continue to death.

35

Pseudo-Theano, *Letter to Eubule* (Alfons Städele, *Die Briefe des Pythagoras und der Pythagoreer*, 166–168)

I hear that you are spoiling your children. A good mother's responsibility is not to provide for her children's pleasure, but to lead them to temperance. Be careful, then, not to act like a mother who does not love her children but flatters them. For when pleasure is children's close companion it makes them undisciplined. For what gratifies young people more than a pleasure to which they have become accustomed? Children, my friend, should be properly reared and not perverted. Their rearing is a perversion of their nature when their souls are given over to pleasure and their bodies indulged, when their souls flee hardships and their bodies become soft.

You must also train young children against those things which frighten them even if it causes them grief and pain. Your purpose in doing so should be that they might not become slaves to these emotions, gluttonous for pleasure and timid about pain, but might honor the good above all by avoiding the former and continuing in the latter. Nor should you make them fond of gorging themselves on food, indulging in pleasures and being totally undisciplined in their games; you should not permit them to say or do whatever they please. Yet you are fearful when they cry and pride yourself when they laugh—and if they hit their nurse and speak disrespectfully to you, you laugh indulgently and keep them cool in summer and warm in winter and provide them with other luxuries. Poor children experience none of these things and are reared more easily; they do not grow less, but are in a much better condition.

You nurse your children like the offspring of Sardanapalus [legendary Assyrian king who epitomized a life given to pleasure], thereby enfeebling the boys' nature with pleasure. For what are you to do with a child who cries when he does not get to eat right away, and when he does eat looks for the delicious dishes, who passes out when it is warm, is ready to drop when it is cold, strikes back when someone rebukes him, is offended when someone does not cater to his pleasure, is peeved when he is not chewing, plays tricks on others to entertain himself, and stumbles around stammering?

So, take care, dear friend. Since you know that spoilt children grow up to become slaves of pleasure, keep such pleasures away from them and rear them austerely and not luxuriously, allow them to experience hunger and thirst, cold and heat, and let them learn respect for their peers and seniors. For in this way they will turn out to be noble in soul whether they are extolled or rebuked. Hardships, my friend, are a kind of preparatory astringent to the children with a view to the virtue that will come to full maturity; when the children have been sufficiently steeped in them they hold the dye of virtue more properly. Watch out, then, my friend, lest, just as badly tended grapevines bear no fruit, so also your children because of your pampering produce the evil of lewdness and worthlessness.

EPITOMES

Epitomes are systematic summaries of larger works or of treatments of subjects. They were composed in virtually all fields of learning and in many literary forms. An epitome could be organized in many different ways—for example, as a summary of a philosopher's system of thought presented according to the traditional threefold division of philosophy into logic, physics, and ethics. It could also be a systematic description of one of these. In early Christian literature, the Sermon on the Mount (Matthew 5–7) and the Sermon on the Plain (Luke 6:20–49) are in the nature of epitomes.

36 The epitome of Hierocles (second century A.D.) is a summary of Stoic ethics. It is preserved in selections published by the anthologist Stobaeus (fifth century A.D.). The precise content and the order in which the subjects were taken up by Hierocles are uncertain, because Stobaeus may have exercised freedom in extracting and organizing his material. The work appears to have been a handbook **(60)**, and, like other epitomes, it may have been used in introductory studies in philosophy in schools. The style, with its frequent repetitions, constant enumeration of points, references to earlier mention of a topic, and the popular level of Stoicism it contains, calls to mind nothing so much as fairly elementary lectures on social ethics, and the lecture hall may indeed have been where it originated. The subjects constitute the usual list of duties *(Haustafel)* toward the gods, one's fatherland, parents, friends, and relatives **(4, 50, 51;** cf. Eph. 5:22–6:9; Col. 3:18–4:1; Titus 2:1–10; 1 Peter 2:13–3:12; *1 Clem.* 1.3; 21.6–9; Ignatius, *Pol.* 4–5; Polycarp, *Phil.* 4–5), as well as common topics (topoi; see pp. 144–161) on friendship and marriage. It is noteworthy that Hierocles is not as interested in these fragments in specifying particular duties as he is in providing the warrants or justifications for the duties he assumes to be commonly known and accepted. However, his complete treatment of each subject has not been preserved. Hierocles is important for the history of late Stoicism and has been a major source for the study of the *Haustafeln.* For these reasons, and since no modern English translation is readily available, an unusually long selection is included in this volume. The Greek text is that edited by C. Wachsmuth (Vols. 1–2) and O. Hense (Vols. 3–5), *Ioannis Stobaei Anthologium* (repr.; Berlin: Weidmann, 1974).

36a Hierocles' treatment of the topos on one's duty to the gods is almost entirely an affirmation of the divine as the source of virtue. All other aspects of one's conduct toward them is to be informed by this conviction. The gods are immutable (cf. Heb. 13:8) in their judgments and do not cause evil (cf. 1 Cor. 10:13; James 1:13–14). On the contrary, God furnishes people with every good they are willing to receive (cf. 2 Peter 1:3–7); evils are the result of our voluntary choice. Divine punishment, too, is an expression not only of the gods' justice but of their desire to bring the erring to repentance (cf. 2 Cor. 7:10; Heb. 12: 5–11; contrast Rom. 2:4; 2 Peter 3:9) and to provide an incentive to others to do so (cf. 1 Cor. 10:6, 11).

Hierocles, *On Duties.* How to Conduct Oneself Toward the Gods (1.3.53–54=1.63, 6–64, 14; 2.9.7=2.181, 8–182, 30 Wachsmuth)

1.3.53–54. One must take into consideration as well the following concerning the gods, namely, that they are immutable and fixed in their judgments, so that they never veer from their original decrees. For there is one immutable and firm virtue which we may reasonably suppose belongs above all to the gods, and which imparts the unfailing and settled quality to the decrees which they have once and for all made. Hence it is clearly not probable that the punishments which the divinity decreed for some people will be remitted. For in fact it is easy to reason further that if the gods change their own decisions and forgo punishing the person they had determined to punish, they would neither be governing the world well and justly, nor would they be able to make a reasonable case for repentance. Poetry also seems to have said such things offhandedly and without reason:

Their hearts by incense and reverent vows and libations and the savour of sacrifice do men turn from wrath with supplication, whenso any man transgresseth and doeth sin [Homer, *Iliad* 9.499–501],

and,

Nay, even the very gods can bend [Homer, *Iliad* 9.497],

and, in short, whatever of a similar nature has been said by the poets.

We should certainly not neglect noting that, even though the gods are not the causes of evil, they attach some evils to certain people and surround those who deserve corporal punishment and loss of their property. They do this not because of malice, thinking that man of necessity must live in distress, but for the sake of punishment. For just as pestilence and drought, and also deluges of rain, earthquakes, and everything of this kind are for the most part produced by certain other physical causes, but at times are caused by the gods when it is critical that the sins of the masses be punished publicly and generally, so also in the same way the gods sometimes afflict an individual's body or cause him to lose his property in order to punish him and to turn others and make them choose what is better.

2.9.7. I think that comprehending that the divine is never the cause of any evil contributes greatly to proper conduct toward the gods. Evils issue from vice alone, but the gods are of themselves the causes of good and of what is useful, yet we do not admit their beneficence but surround ourselves with voluntary evils. It appears to me at this point that the poet already has said it well, namely that "mortals blame the gods," as if they caused their evils, "but they even of themselves, through their own blind folly, have sorrows beyond that which is ordained" [Homer, *Odyssey* 1.32, 33, 34]. One might conclude from many arguments that God is never in any way the cause of evil, but for the present Plato's statement will suffice, namely, "it is not the property of heat to chill, but of its opposite; nor of one who is beneficent to harm, but of its opposite" [*Republic* 1.335D]. Moreover, God is good, and has been naturally filled from the beginning with all virtues, so he could not do evil or cause anyone to do evil. On the contrary, he furnishes every good to all people who are willing to receive it, and, in addition to the good, he freely bestows on us, of those things which are intermediate [be-

tween vice and virtue], that which is according to nature as
well as that which produces what is according to nature.
The one sole cause of evil is vice.

This we must understand, that the gods are the cause of
good, and vice of evil. What, then, are the causes of our
suffering? Since some of the intermediate things are against
nature and disadvantageous or, by Zeus, are efficient causes
of things which are, it is worth our now forming a judgment
about them, for example, about disease, mutilation, death,
poverty, reputation, and the like. Vice brings many of them
to their natural end; because of a lack of self-control and
lustfulness many diseases are produced, and many mutilations; because of injustice many people have had their hands
cut off and received other such mutilations, and many have
actually died. Indeed, humane medicine is frequently ob-
structed by vice from attaining its goal, for the remedies of
the art become unsuccessful because of the disobedience
and lack of self-control and the aversion to work of those
who are ill. Moreover, profligacy and extravagance have
made many people poor and needy, and greed and meanness many disreputable. Next to vice matter is the second
cause of these things. For some things are high above us, as
though they had come forth from the purest substance and
are moving evenly while all things in them are accomplished
according to the principles of nature. But others are earthly
exactly as if they had sediment and mud as the substance of
nature.

36b Moralists frequently stressed the unitary view of society, sometimes describing the household as the beginning of the city or
providing the seeds for the constitution (**36g**). Hierocles does
so by developing the popular body metaphor (**63**) and by view-
ing public and private morality from the perspective of the
well-being of the state (cf. 1 Tim. 3:1–2; Titus 3:1; 1 Peter
2:13–17). His deep respect for the laws is expressed by calling
them secondary gods of a sort (for the expression, see also **36c**;
cf. Mark 12:13–17; Rom. 13:1–7; *1 Clem.* 60.4–61.2; Polycarp,
Phil. 12.3). His even higher estimation of the ancestral customs
and his corresponding suspicion of innovation reflect the period's high evaluation of continuity and tradition (contrast
Matt. 15:1–9; 1 Peter 1:18–19).

Hierocles, *On Duties*. How to Conduct Oneself Toward One's Fatherland (3.39.34–36=3.730, 17–734, 10 Hense)

After discussing the gods, it is most reasonable to set forth how to conduct oneself toward one's fatherland [*patris*]. For, by Zeus, it is as it were some second god, and our first and greatest parent. Hence he who gave it a name did not do so inappropriately; he formed a derivative [from "father"], but gave it a feminine ending so that it might be a sort of mixture of "father" and "mother." This word also dictates that we honor our one fatherland equally with our two parents, that we prefer it to either of our two parents separately, and that we not honor the two together more than it, but that we respect them equally. There is still another reason which exhorts us to honor it more than our two parents together, and not only them, but together with them, to honor it more than our wives, children and friends, in short, more than all other things.

The person who prefers one finger to the five is stupid, but he who prefers the five to the one is most reasonable, for the former esteems lightly even the preferred finger, while the latter in the five preserves also the single finger. In the same way, that person also is stupid who wishes to save himself more than his fatherland, and in addition acts unlawfully and desires the impossible, while he who honors his fatherland more than himself is dear to the gods and firm in his reasoning. Nevertheless, it has been said that even if one were not numbered with the system but were examined separately, it is fitting that he prefer the preservation of the system rather than his own. For the destruction of the city shows that there is no preservation of the citizen, in the same way that the destruction of the hand involves the destruction of the finger as part of the hand. Let us then sum up, that we should not separate what is publicly profitable from what is privately profitable, but to consider them one and the same. For what is profitable to the fatherland is common to each of its parts, since the whole without its parts is nothing. And what is profitable to the citizen is also fitting to the city, if indeed it is taken to be profitable to the citizen. For what is of advantage to a dancer as a dancer would also be of advantage to the entire chorus. So, if we store all this reasoning in our minds we

shall have much light on particulars and shall on no occasion neglect our duty to our fatherland.

Because of this, I say, the person who would conduct
himself well toward his fatherland should get rid of every
passion and disease of the soul. He should also observe the
laws of the fatherland as secondary gods of a kind and be
guided by them, and, if someone should attempt to transgress them or introduce innovations we should with all dil-
igence prevent him and in every way possible oppose him.
For it is not beneficial to a city if its laws are dishonored
and new things are preferred to the old. We should therefore prevent those who are stubbornly set on doing this
from casting their votes and initiating violent change. I
therefore approve of Zaleucus, the Locrian lawgiver, who
decreed that a person who wishes to introduce a new law
should do so with a rope around his neck so that he could
be strangled on the spot if he did not change the original
constitution of the state to the greater advantage of the
community. No less than the laws should we also guard the
customs which are truly those of the fatherland and are
perhaps older than the laws themselves. But those customs
which date from yesterday or the day before and are now
introduced into every city should not be regarded as customs of the fatherland, and perhaps not as customs at all.
In the next place, custom is an unwritten law of a sort,
inscribed by a good lawgiver, namely the approval of those
who follow it, and perhaps approximate those things which
are naturally just.

36c In the topos on marriage (**36g**), Hierocles stresses the advantage of having children who can benefit their elders. Here he
views children's exercise of their responsibility as a reciproca-
tion for what they have received from their parents (**36d**; cf.
Matt. 15:5–6; 1 Tim. 5:4, 8; contrast 2 Cor. 12:14), whose
physical and spiritual needs should be met by their children.
That the emphasis is on the children's responsibility is to be
expected in this topos, but it presupposes that the parents
also have responsibilities (cf. Eph. 6:1–4; Col. 3:20–21) and
that, like the gods to men, they are beneficent to their children.
This fragment specifies, more than the others, particular
duties.

Hierocles, *On Duties*. How to Conduct Oneself Toward One's Parents (4.25.53 = 4.640, 4–644, 15 Hense)

After discussing the gods and the fatherland, what person should be mentioned before our parents? We must then speak about them. We won't err in saying that they are secondary and earthly gods of a sort and, if it is lawful to say so, on account of their nearness to us we honor them more highly than the gods. But we must begin with the assumption that the only measure of our gratitude to them is perpetual and unyielding eagerness to repay their beneficence, since, even if we were to do a great deal for them, that would still be far too inadequate. Yet even these deeds are almost theirs, since they made us who perform them. So, if the works of Phidias or other artists should themselves produce other works of art we would not hesitate to ascribe these too to the artists. In the same way we might reasonably say that our accomplishments are the deeds of our parents who brought us into existence. It is not the case that we perform some deeds while our parents who brought us into existence perform others.

So, in order to choose our duties to them easily, we should always have this summary statement at hand, namely, that our parents are the images of the gods, and, by Zeus, domestic gods, benefactors, kinsmen, creditors, lords, and the firmest of friends. For they are images most like the gods, made far superior to the ephemeral power of the artists. They guard our homes and live with us and are, furthermore, our greatest benefactors, supplying us with the most important things, indeed, by Zeus, not only the things that we do have, but also those which they wished to give us and for which they themselves pray. In addition, they are our nearest kinsmen and the causes of our relationship with other people. They are lenders of the most valuable things, and take back only things which will benefit us when we repay them. For what gain is so great to a child as piety and gratitude to his parents? They are, indeed, most justly our lords. For whose possession would we rather be than those through whom we exist? Moreover, they are constant and unbidden friends and comrades, allies on all occasions and in all circumstances. But since the name of parent is the most eminent of all the ones that have been mentioned, and is what we call the gods themselves, we should add something else to this notion, namely, that we should acknowledge that we live in our father's house as if we were attendants and priests of sorts in a temple, appointed and consecrated by nature itself, and entrusted with our parents' care. By distinguishing between the care of the body and the soul, by showing the utmost concern for each of them separately, and by being willing to heed reason, we shall fulfil our duty.

Our discussion of the body is brief, but necessary. We should liberally provide food for them which is adapted to the weakness that comes with old age, and in addition, bed, sleep, unguents, a bath, clothing, in short, all bodily necessities, so that they may never want for any of these things. In this way we shall imitate their care in rearing us when we were newly born. Hence, we should force ourselves to apply a prophetic element to their care by seeking to discover what particular things they desire which pertain to the body, whether they mention them or not. For they too divined much about us when we frequently let it be known in inarticulate and sobbing sounds that we needed something but were unable to make clear what it was that we needed. So by earlier supplying our needs, they have become our teachers, instructing us in what they deserve to receive from us.

As to their souls, we should first afford them cheerfulness, which will especially be produced, if nothing prevents us, by associating with them night and day, and as we walk, are anointed, and live with them. Just as people are cheered by their association with family and friends as though it were a procession which escorts them on their way, so also parents who are about to depart from life are particularly gratified by and hold dear the close attention their children pay them. Nevertheless, if at any time they should make a mistake, as those brought up in a more vulgar way frequently do, we should correct them, but not, by Zeus, by rebuking them the way we do our subordinates or peers, but by exhorting them, and then not as though they had erred in ignorance, but as though through inattention they had committed an oversight which they certainly would not have had they been more attentive. For admonitions, especially those which are drawn out, are painful to old people, and their oversight should therefore be cured with exhortations and a certain ingeniousness. Children also contribute to their parents' joy by performing even seemingly servile duties such as washing their feet, making their beds, and standing ready to wait on them. For they get no little enjoyment when they receive the necessary services from the dearest hands and use their own offspring as servants. And it will especially please parents that their children are seen to honor those whom they love and consider highly. Children should therefore love their parents' relatives and consider them worthy of care, as they also should their parents' friends and in fact all whom they hold dear. With this as starting point we also gain a conception of many other duties which are in no way small or casual. For since our parents are pleased by the care we bestow on those they love, and they especially love us, it is evident that we would in no casual way please them if we took care of ourselves.

36d The subject of brotherly love, widely discussed in popular morality, is most systematically treated by Plutarch in his tractate *On Brotherly Love*. Hierocles restricts himself to common precepts and metaphors which normally describe social relationships, but which he briefly develops and applies to the relationship between brothers. The principle that is basic to family (**36c, 50**), and indeed to all social relationships, is for him the Golden Rule (cf. Matt. 7:12; Luke 6:31), which represents the popular moral ideal of reciprocity. He warns against self-love (cf. 2 Tim. 3:2), retaliation (cf. Matt. 5:39–42; 1 Peter 2:23), and making friends of strangers rather than brothers (contrast Gal. 6:10). While one could with profit exhort a brother (cf. 2 Thess. 3:15), his wildness should be overcome with beneficence (cf. Rom. 12:21). Hierocles describes the relationship that should exist between brothers with an extended body image (**63;** cf. 1 Cor. 12:12–26). In the New Testament, brotherly love describes spiritual rather than blood relationship, and introduces paraenesis on relationships within the community. Used in this sense, brotherly love or relationship between brothers is also connected with body imagery and nonretaliation (Rom. 12:3–21; cf. 1 Cor. 6:1–8; 1 Peter 3:8–9).

Hierocles, *On Duties*. On Fraternal Love (4.27.20=4.660, 15–664, 18 Hense)

The first bit of advice, therefore, is very clear, easily obtained, and common to all people. For it is a sound word which everyone will recognize as clear: Treat anybody what-

soever as though you supposed that he were you and you he.
For someone would treat even a servant well if he pondered
how he would want to be treated if the slave were the master
and he the slave. Something similar can also be said of parents with respect to their children, of children with respect
to their parents, and, in short, of all people with respect to
all others. The precept is singularly adapted to the common
topic of brothers, since the man who is considering how to
treat his brother need begin with no other presupposition
than promptly to assume their natural sameness.

Let this, then, be the first admonition, that a man should
deal with his brother in the same way he would expect his
brother to deal with him. "But, by Zeus," someone will say,
"I am a man of moderation and a gentleman, but my brother
is gauche and unsociable." But that would not be putting it
correctly. In the first place, perhaps he does not speak the
truth, for self-love is sufficient to make one magnify and
greatly glorify one's own qualities while diminishing and
bad-mouthing those of other people. Frequently, therefore,
because of self-love inferior people prefer themselves to
others who are much superior to them. In the next place,
even if your brother should be such a person, I would say,
"Prove yourself better than him," "Overcome his wildness
with beneficence." For those who deal moderately with reasonable people deserve no great thanks, but to calm a stupid, gauche person by what is done to him is the accomplishment of a real man and deserves much praise. In fact,
exhortation is not at all ineffective, for even in people with
the most absurd dispositions there are seeds of change to a
better condition, and of honor and love for their benefactors. For do not even wild animals, which are by nature
hostile to the human race, and are only led by force after first
being placed in chains and confined in cages, do not even
they later become domesticated when they are tamed by
certain kinds of attention and daily food? And will not the
man who is a brother, or even someone who is in no way
related, who in every respect deserves attention much more,
not change to a milder disposition, even if he should not
completely forsake his excessive roughness? With respect to
every person, then, and especially a brother, we should imitate Socrates who, when someone said to him, "May I die if
I do not avenge myself on you," replied, "May I die if I do
not make you my friend." But so much for that.

In the next place, we should consider that in a certain way a person's brothers are parts of him just as my eyes are of me, and similarly my hands, and the rest. Family relationships are similar. If the eyes and hands, therefore, should each receive its own soul and mind, they would treat the rest with respect in every way possible on account of the partnership we have mentioned before, because they would not be able to perform their own functions without the presence of the other members. In the same way also, we who are men and admit to having a soul should in no way relax the esteem with which we should deal with our brothers. Furthermore, brothers far more than parts of the body are adapted by nature to help each other. For the eyes, indeed, being present with each other, see together, and one hand works together with the other that is present. But the cooperation of brothers with each other is much more varied, for they do things which by common consent are excellent even if they should be completely separated from each other, and they greatly benefit each other even if the distance that separates them is immense. On the whole, we must consider that our lives appear to be a long sort of war which lasts many years, partly because of the nature of things themselves which possess a certain resistant quality, and partly because of the sudden and unexpected incursions of fortune, but especially because of vice itself, which does not abstain from any violence or from guile and evil stratagems. Hence nature, not ignorant of the purpose for which it produced us, brought each of us forth accompanied, in a certain manner, by a body of allies. No one, therefore, is alone, nor is he born "from an oak or a stone" [Homer, *Odyssey* 19.163], but from parents and in conjunction with brothers, kindred, and other members of the household.

This proposition is helpful to us, for it wins over to us strangers and people who are in no way related to us by blood, and supplies us with an abundance of allies. We are therefore by nature eager to embrace anyone whomsoever and make him our friend. Hence it is pure madness to wish to form friendships with people who have no natural affection for us, and voluntarily to form the most intimate relationships with them possible, and yet to neglect those ready helpers and allies who are supplied by nature itself, who happen to be brothers.

36e The title of the topos from which this fragment was excerpted
may lead one to expect detailed advice on relationships with
one's various kinsfolk. Once more, however, Hierocles sacrifices prescriptions on matters of detail in favor of a description that locates the immediate family at the center of society.
All other social relationships extend outward from it in con-
centric circles until all humanity is embraced. One's distant kin
are closer to this center but, like the other circles, must also be
transferred from the larger circles to the smaller. One of the
ways to demonstrate esteem for them is to extend the designa-
tion of father, mother, and brother to people actually more
distantly related (cf. Philemon 15–16; 1 Thess. 1:4; 2 Thess.
2:13; 1 Cor. 5:11; 6:1–6).

**Hierocles, *On Duties*. How to Conduct Oneself Toward
One's Kinsfolk (4.27.23=4.671, 3–673, 18 Hense)**

It is consistent with what has been said about our treatment
of our parents, brothers, wives and children, to add a statement about our relatives. It has some things in common with
that earlier discussion and for that reason can be given concisely. In short, each of us is, as it were, circumscribed by
many circles, some of which are smaller and others larger,
some of which enclose and others which are enclosed, according to the different and unequal relationships that they
have with each other. The first circle, which is also the most
closely drawn, is the one someone himself draws around his
mind as a center, and in it the body and whatever is admitted
for its sake are enclosed. This, I dare say, is the smallest
circle and all but touches the center. The second circle,
which is farther from the center, encloses the first, and in it
parents, brothers, wife, and children are arranged. The third
circle from the center contains uncles and aunts, grandfathers and grandmothers, and also our brothers' and sisters'
children. Next is the circle which encloses the remaining
relatives. Then comes the one which encloses the common
people, and after it the one with members of the same tribe,
then the one with citizens, and finally, in this manner, the
circle of those who live near the city, and the one of people
of the same race. But the outermost and largest circle which
encloses all the circles is that of the whole human race.
    Viewed thus, the person who has set himself to deal in the
required manner with each of these must gather the circles

in some way, as it were, to the center, and must always eagerly transfer people from the circles which enclose to those which are enclosed. The person who loves his kindred must treat his parents and brothers well and, on the same analogy, also his older relatives of both sexes, such as grandfathers or grandmothers, and uncles and aunts; those of his own age, such as his cousins; and those younger than himself, such as his cousins' children.

We have thus provided clear counsel on how we should deal with our relatives, after having earlier taught how we should treat ourselves, our parents, and brothers, and in addition, our wives and children. To this should be added that we should likewise honor those from the third circle as well as their relatives. For something will be subtracted from the goodwill towards those far removed from us by blood; nevertheless, we should be most eager that they be assimilated to us. For this distance will become moderate if through our initiative we shorten the distance in our relationship with each individual. Now, we have said what is comprehensive and most prudent.

We must also add a statement on our use of names, when we call cousins, uncles and aunts by the names of brothers, fathers and mothers, and our other relatives, some uncles, others nephews and nieces, and others cousins, if, on account of the way names can be extended, their ages allow us to do so. For this way of addressing them would at once be no obscure sign of our esteem for each of them, and would at the same time urge us on and make us strain to contract the circles as I have described. Nevertheless, since we have arrived at this point in our discussion, it is not untimely to call to memory the distinction I made with respect to parents. For in that place where I compared mothers with fathers, I said that we should bestow more familial affection on mothers and more honor on our fathers. In conformity with that, I should here add that it is fitting for us to have more familial affection for relatives on our mothers' side, and to pay greater honor to those on our fathers' side.

36f In this fragment from a very common topos, Hierocles is constrained to correct what he considers too sharp a distinction between the duties of a husband and a wife. He too places the woman over those matters internal (cf. 1 Tim. 5:9–16; *1 Clem.*

1.3) and the husband over those external (cf. 1 Tim. 2:1–7) to the home as the majority did, but he refuses to make the distinction absolute.

Hierocles, *On Duties.* Household Management (4.28.21 = 5.696, 21–699, 15 Hense)

Before anything else I should speak about the occupations by which a household is maintained. They should be divided in the usual manner, namely, to the husband should be assigned those which have to do with agriculture, commerce, and the affairs of the city; to the wife those which have to do with spinning and the preparation of food, in short, those of a domestic nature. It is not right, however, that they should be completely inexperienced in each other's work. For it would on occasion be fitting for the wife, when she is in the country, to supervise the laborers and to take the place of the master of the house; and for the husband to turn his attention to domestic affairs, to inquire about some things and to oversee others that are taking place. If they shared with each other in these necessary cares, what pertains to their partnership would thereby be more firmly bound. Since, however, we have arrived at this point in our discussion, I think I should not omit mentioning manual labor, since it is reasonable to add the following to what has been said about the occupations.

Why, then, is it necessary to say that it is fitting for a man to engage in agricultural labors? For there are not many people who are not persuaded of this. Though there is so much luxury and idleness in life today, it is nevertheless rare to find a man who is not willing and eager to participate in the work of sowing and planting as well as the other agricultural chores. Perhaps, however, the argument which encourages a man to engage in the occupations assigned to women will be much less persuasive. Men who are very clean and neat in their appearance are not disposed to engage in spinning, since, for the most part, it is cheap little men and the tribe of those who are weak and effeminate who emulate female softness and lower themselves to working with wool. It is not seemly that a real man apply himself to such things. So, as for myself, I would perhaps not advise those who have not provided strong proof of their masculinity and self-control to engage in any such occupation. Nevertheless, if a man throughout his entire life has rid himself of all unnatural suspicion, what will hinder him from sharing in them with his wife? For is it not thought that more of the other domestic occupations are fitting for men than for women? For they are more toilsome and require bodily strength, for example, grinding, kneading bread, cutting wood, drawing water, moving large vessels around, shaking out bedclothes, and everything else on that order. It would be sufficient that these duties be performed by husbands, but it is also fitting that something be added to the wife, so that she may not only participate with her maids in spinning, but may also apply herself to other more manly occupations. For it seems to me that preparing food, drawing water, lighting fires, making beds, and every similar chore are the proper occupations of a freeborn woman. But a wife would appear much more beautiful to her husband, especially if she is young and not yet worn out by pregnancies, if she too would participate in harvesting grapes and gathering olives, and, if he permits, in sowing, ploughing, and handing him his tools for digging and planting. When a household is governed in this way by a husband and wife by virtue of their occupations it appears to me that in this respect it would be conducted in the best manner.

36g Hierocles represents the view of other Stoics that men should marry. However, the arguments that he marshals and explicit statements that he makes indicate that there was no unanimity on all questions touching marriage. His first reason for marrying is that there can be no cities if there are no households (**36b**), and households are imperfect without marriage. In contrast to some philosophers, including other Stoics, he holds that as marriage is to be preferred by the wise man, so it should also be by others. He rejects the view that it is burdensome (cf. 1 Cor. 7:8–9, 28), claiming that it is only burdensome when men marry for the wrong reason. Nature furthermore teaches us to marry, and reason enables us to determine what is in harmony with nature. The real purpose for marrying, however, is to have and rear children (**35**; cf. 1 Tim. 2:15; 5:14), and he therefore condemns the practice of exposing infants. Children are helpers to their parents and grandparents (**36c**) and ensure the stability of the state. Even without children, however, marriage is advantageous because of the companionship a solicitous wife affords (contrast 1 Cor. 7:32–35). Marriage partners are yoked together by fate, consecrated to the gods (cf. Matt. 19:3–6; 1 Thess. 4:3–8). United in body and soul (38), they apparently together are to manage their household as friends (cf. 1 Tim. 3:5, 12; 5:14).

Hierocles, *On Duties.* On Marriage (4.22.21–24=4.502, 1–507, 5 Hense; 24.14=4.603, 8–605 Hense)

22.21–24. It is most necessary to speak about marriage. For our whole race is naturally adapted to partnership, and the first and most elementary of partnerships is that brought about by marriage. For there would be no cities if there were no households; yet the household of an unmarried man is truly imperfect, while that of a married man is perfect and full.

Hence we have demonstrated in the treatise "On Households" that the married life is to be preferred by the wise man, but life without a wife is not, except in special circumstances. So, since we should imitate the man of intellect in those things we can, and marriage is preferred by him, it is evident that it would also be fitting to us except some circumstance prevent us. This is the first point.

But it seems that even before the wise man, nature, which also excites the wise man himself to marry, urges us to do so. Nature not only made us gregarious, but also disposed us to live in pairs, and enjoined that copulation have one purpose, I mean the procreation of children and a steady way of life. Nature justly teaches that we should choose what is fitting and in harmony with the condition it has given us. Every animal, therefore, lives in harmony with its own natural constitution, and, by Zeus, every plant likewise lives according to the life enjoined on plants. Nevertheless, plants use no reasoning or enumeration in selecting what they examine, but use mere nature since they have no share in soul; animals on the other hand make use of impressions which draw them and drive them to what is proper to them. But to us nature gave reason in order that it might explore all other things, and together with them, or rather before them, might explore nature itself so that, fixed on it as a bright and stable target, and choosing what is in harmony with it, reason might cause us to live in a manner that in every way befits nature.

Hence no one will err in saying that a household is imperfect without marriage, for it is impossible to conceive of what governs without what is governed, or of what is governed without what governs. This argument especially appears to me to put to shame those persons who are prejudiced against marriage.

I affirm, therefore, that marriage is also advantageous, in the first place, because it bears a truly divine fruit in the procreation of children. Seeing that they are united to us by nature, children are our helpers in all our undertakings while we still enjoy full strength, they are good allies when we are hard pressed in the prime of life and depressed by old age, they are fitting participants in our joy when we do well, and in times of adversity with sympathy they provide relief from our griefs.

And yet, living with a wife even before the birth of children is advantageous. For in the first place, when we are worn out by laboring out of doors, she solicitously entertains us by restoring and refreshing us with the greatest of care. In the next place, she makes us forget our problems. For those gloomy circumstances of life which involve the forum or the gymnasium or the country or, in general, all our anxieties while we are occupied with our friends and spend time with our associates are at the time not obvious to us, since they are obscured by inevitable distractions. But when we are freed from them and return home and our souls are, so to speak, at leisure, they approach and use this opportunity to torment us at the time when our lives are empty of goodwill and lonesome. But when a wife is present she becomes a great comfort in these circumstances by asking her husband about non-domestic matters or by bringing up and considering together with him matters concerning the home, thus causing him to relax, and she cheers him up by her unaffected enthusiasm.

It would make this discussion too long to go through all the details one after the other and describe how capable she is at festivals when she takes joint charge of sacrifices and offerings; how capable during her husband's travels abroad when she keeps the household stable and does not leave it entirely without someone in charge; how capable in taking care of servants; how capable a helper in times of illness. It is sufficient to say by way of summary that all men need two things for a moderate way of life, namely the help of kinfolk and sympathetic goodwill. But we shall find nothing more sympathetic than a wife nor anything more closely related than children. Both of these marriage provides. How, then, can it not be the most advantageous thing to us?

I also think that a married life is beautiful. For what else could be such an adornment as the association between a husband and wife? It is not luxurious houses, walls encased in marble, peristyles decorated with stones which are admired by people who are ignorant of goodness, nor paintings and clipped myrtle groves, nor anything else which astounds the foolish, which is the beauty of a family. Rather, the beauty of a household consists in the yoking together of a husband and wife who are united to each other by fate, are consecrated to the gods who preside over weddings, births, and houses, agree with each other and have all things in common, including their bodies, or rather their souls, and who exercise appropriate rule over their household and servants, take care in rearing their children, and pay an attention to the necessities of life which is neither intense nor slack, but moderate and fitting. For what could be "greater and better," as the most admirable Homer says, "than when husband and wife live at home with one accord" [*Odyssey* 6.183]?

I have therefore frequently marveled at those men who think that married life is burdensome. For a wife, by Zeus, is not a burden or a load, as they think, but on the contrary, she is something light and easily borne, or rather, she has the ability to relieve her husband of things that are truly annoying and burdensome. For there is nothing so burdensome that it cannot easily be borne together by a husband and wife if they are of one mind and wish to do so. But imprudence is truly burdensome and insufferable to those who have acquired it, for through it things that are naturally light become burdensome, among others, even a wife. In reality, to many marriage is intolerable, not because it is intrinsically so, nor because the association with a wife is naturally so. But when we marry women we should not, and in addition are ourselves entirely inexperienced in life and are unprepared to take a wife in the way a freeborn woman should be taken, then it happens that the association with her becomes difficult and intolerable.

Doubtlessly marriage does turn out to be intolerable for many men. For they do not take wives for the sake of procreating children and sharing their lives with their wives, but some marry because of the size of her dowry, others because of her beautiful figure, and others for other such reasons. By using these bad advisers they seek no knowledge of the bride's disposition and manner but celebrate the wedding to their own destruction; and with their doors decked out with garlands they introduce into their homes a tyrant instead of a wife, and do it however incapable they are of standing up to her and competing with her for first place.

It is clear, then, that it is because of these things and not because of itself that marriage is intolerable to many. We should not, as the saying goes, lay blame on things to which no blame attaches, nor should we turn our own weakness and our ignorance in using them into complaints against them. Besides, it is also otherwise most unreasonable to search on all sides for the resources of friendship and to procure for ourselves some friends and associates who will be our allies against life's vexations, but to hate the alliance and help given us by nature, the laws, and the gods, which we receive from a wife and children.

24.14 In the topos on marriage and the procreation of children we shall also treat the subject of having many children. It is in some way according to nature, and in conformity with marriage, that all or at least most of the children who are born should be reared. But for a quite improper reason many seem not to heed this advice; they are disposed not to do so out of love of wealth and because they think that poverty is an exceedingly great evil.

In the first place, then, we should consider that in children we not only beget for ourselves helpers, persons who will take care of us in our old age, and who will share with us in every fortune and circumstance; we beget them not only on our own behalf, but in many ways also for our parents. For the procreation of children pleases them since, if we should suffer some calamity before they die we would leave them someone to take care of them in their old age. It is a beautiful thing for a grandfather to be led by the hand by his grandchildren and to be considered by them as deserving of other care. So, in the first place, we should please our own parents by taking care to have children. In the next place, we shall cooperate with the prayers and fervent wishes of those who begot us. For from the very first they attended to our birth, intending to have a very large issue and to leave behind a succession of children's children, and they planned our marriage, procreation, and rearing. Hence, by marrying and begetting children we shall, as it were, answer part of their prayers, but, if we hold contrary opinions, we shall thwart their deliberate choice. Moreover, it appears that everyone who voluntarily and without some prohibiting circumstance declines to marry and beget children accuses his parents of madness, as not having examined marriage with right reasoning.

The inconsistency in this is easily detected. For how can a person not completely contradict himself when, on the one hand, he finds pleasure in life and continues in it as one who was fittingly brought to life by his parents, but, on the other, supposes that for him to beget others is one of the things he must reject? In the first place, as I have said, we should keep in mind that we beget children not only for ourselves, but also for those for whose sakes we ourselves were begotten, and in the next place, for our friends and relatives. For it pleases them too to see our children, both because of goodwill and friendship, but also because of the security that children provide. For the lives of those who have relatives are moored like ships which, though they are tossed by the waves, are firmly secured by many anchors. Therefore, the man who loves his relatives and friends is eager to marry and have children.

Our country especially urges us to do so. For I dare say that we raise children not so much for ourselves as for our country by planning for the constitution of the state that follows us and supplying the community with our successors. Hence the priest should know that he owes priests to his country, the ruler rulers, the public orator public orators, and, in short, the citizen citizens. So, just as to a chorus the continuation of its members is gratifying, and to an army that of its soldiers, so also to a city the continuation of its citizens is gratifying. If a city were a constitution of short duration and its life commensurate with man's, it would need no succession. But since it extends to many generations and, if it enjoys good fortune, continues as a city for many ages, it is clear that we should aim not only at the present, but also the future, that we should not neglect our country and leave it desolate, but should, in consequence of our children, leave it well established in hope.

COMPILATIONS

Under compilations are included collections of material that differ from epitomes (see pp. 85–104) in not being as systematic in their organization. Wide use was made of a great variety of compilations, the numerous editions and permutations of which reached their high point in the Byzantine period. These compilations are valuable resources for the history of philosophy and literature for two main reasons: they sometimes contain evidence of philosophers' views that are otherwise unknown and they sometimes include allusions to or quotations from literary works that have been lost. Their main goals were the practical ones of education and moral formation, hence the majority of them contain material that could easily be memorized.

SUMMARIES OF A PHILOSOPHER'S TEACHING

The sayings attributed to Epicurus, thought to represent the capstone of his ethical theory (cf. Matt. 19:18–19), are on occasion more discursive than some of the other philosophers' sayings that have been collected. Nevertheless, Epicurus' habit of deliberately casting his teachings in forms to aid memorization is also evidenced in these sayings. Diogenes Laertius appends these sayings to his account of Epicurus' life, in which he elsewhere supplements his biographical sketch with information from such sources as anecdotes and Epicurus' own letters.

37

Epicurus, *The Principal Doctrines* 5–17 (Diogenes Laertius, *Lives of Eminent Philosophers* 10.140–144)

It is impossible to live a pleasant life without living wisely and well and justly, and it is impossible to live wisely and well and justly without living pleasantly. Whenever any one of these is lacking, when, for instance, the man is not able to live wisely, though he lives well and justly, it is impossible for him to live a pleasant life.

In order to obtain security from other men any means whatsoever of procuring this was a natural good.

Some men have sought to become famous and renowned, thinking that thus they would make themselves secure against their fellow-men. If, then, the life of such persons really was secure, they attained natural good; if, however, it was insecure, they have not attained the end which by nature's own prompting they originally sought.

No pleasure is in itself evil, but the things which produce certain pleasures entail annoyances many times greater than the pleasures themselves.

If all pleasure had been capable of accumulation,—if this had gone on not only by recurrence in time, but all over the frame or, at any rate, over the principal parts of man's nature, there would never have been any difference between one pleasure and another, as in fact there is.

If the objects which are productive of pleasures to profligate persons really freed them from fears of the mind,—the fears, I mean, inspired by celestial and atmospheric phenomena, the fear of death, the fear of pain; if, further, they taught them to limit their desires, we should never have any fault to find with such persons, for they would then be filled with pleasures to overflowing on all sides and would be exempt from all pain, whether of body or mind, that is, from all evil.

If we had never been molested by alarms at celestial and atmospheric phenomena, nor by the misgiving that death somehow affects us, nor by neglect of the proper limits of pains and desires, we should have had no need to study natural science.

It would be impossible to banish fear on matters of the highest importance, if a man did not know the nature of the whole universe, but lived in dread of what the legends tell us. Hence without the study of nature there was no enjoyment of unmixed pleasures.

There would be no advantage in providing security against our fellow-men, so long as we were alarmed by occurrences over our heads or beneath the earth or in general by whatever happens in the boundless universe.

When tolerable security against our fellow-men is attained, then on a basis of power sufficient to afford support and of material prosperity arises in most genuine form the security of a quiet private life withdrawn from the multitude.

Nature's wealth at once has its bounds and is easy to procure; but the wealth of vain fancies recedes to an infinite distance.

Fortune but seldom interferes with the wise man; his

greatest and highest interests have been, are, and will be, directed by reason throughout the course of his life.

The just man enjoys the greatest peace of mind, while the unjust is full of the utmost disquietude.

ADVICE ON A PARTICULAR SUBJECT

Plutarch's precepts on marriage were compiled for a certain couple, Pollianus and Eurydice, who had recently been married. The work illustrates how a compilation could be made for particular purposes. At the beginning of the work, Plutarch acknowledges the conventional nature of his compilation, and the work itself shows the traditional nature of the instruction contained in such compilations—for example, reflection on the nature of unity, responsible conduct in the household as a requirement for public service (cf. 1 Tim. 3:4–5, 12–13), and warnings against ornate adornment (**34;** cf. 1 Peter 3:1–6).

38

Plutarch, *Advice to Bride and Groom* 142E–143A, 144CD, 144F–145D

142E–143A. Philosophers say of bodies that some are composed of separate elements, as a fleet or an army, others of elements joined together, as a house or a ship, and still others form together an intimate union, as is the case with every living creature. In about the same way, the marriage of a couple in love with each other is an intimate union; that of those who marry for dowry or children is of persons joined together, and that of those who merely sleep in the same bed is of separate persons who may be regarded as cohabiting, but not really living together. As the mixing of liquids, according to what men of science say, extends throughout their entire content, so also in the case of married people there ought to be a mutual amalgamation of their bodies, property, friends, and relations. In fact, the purpose of the Roman law-giver who prohibited the giving and receiving of presents between man and wife was, not to prevent their sharing in anything, but that they should feel that they shared all things in common.

144CD. When the orator Gorgias read to the Greeks at Olympia a speech about concord, Melanthius [Athenian poet, fifth century B.C.] said, "This fellow is giving us advice about concord, and yet in his own household he has not prevailed upon himself, his wife, and maidservant, three persons only, to live in concord." For there was, apparently, some love on Gorgias's part and jealousy on the wife's part towards the girl. A man therefore ought to have his household well harmonized who is going to harmonize State, Forum, and friends. For it is much more likely that the sins of women rather than sins against women will go unnoticed by most people.

144F–145D. Plato used to advise the elderly men more especially to have the sense of shame before the young, so that the young may be respectful toward them; for where the old men are without sense of shame, he felt, no respect or deference is engendered in the young. The husband ought to bear this is mind, and show no greater respect for anybody than for his wife, seeing that their chamber is bound to be for her a school of orderly behaviour or of wantonness. The man who enjoys the very pleasures from which he tries to dissuade his wife is in no wise different from him who bids her fight to the death against the enemies to whom he has himself surrendered.

In regard to love of finery, I beg, Eurydice, that you will read and try to remember what was written to Aristylla [unknown person] by Timoxena [Plutarch's wife]; and as for you, Pollianus, you must not think that your wife will refrain from immoderate display and extravagance if she sees that you do not despise these things in others, but, on the contrary, find delight in gilded drinking cups, pictured walls, trappings for mules, and showy neckbands for horses. For it is impossible to expel extravagance from the wife's part of the house when it has free range amid the men's rooms.

Besides, Pollianus, you already possess sufficient maturity to study philosophy, and I beg that you will beautify your character with the aid of discourses which are attended by logical demonstration and mature deliberation, seeking the company and instruction of teachers who will help you. And for your wife you must collect from every source what is useful, as do the bees, and carrying it within your own self impart it to her, and then discuss it with her, and make the best of these doctrines her favourite and familiar themes. For to her "Thou art a father and precious-loved mother, yea, and a brother as well." No less ennobling is it for a man to hear his wife say, "My dear husband, 'Nay, but thou art to me' [Homer, *Iliad* 6.429] guide, philosopher, and teacher in all that is most lovely and divine." Studies of this sort, in the first place, divert women from all untoward conduct; for a woman studying geometry will be ashamed to be a dancer, and she will not swallow any beliefs in magic charms while she is under the charm of Plato's or Xenophon's words. And if anybody professes power to pull down the moon from the sky, she will laugh at the ignorance and stupidity of women who believe these things, inasmuch as she herself is not unschooled in astronomy, and has read in the books about Aglaonice [a magician], the daughter of Hegetor of Thessaly, and how she, through being thoroughly acquainted with the periods of the full moon when it is subject to eclipse, and, knowing beforehand the time when the moon was due to be overtaken by the earth's shadow, imposed upon the women, and made them all believe that she was drawing down the moon.

GNOMES

Pithy sayings or maxims were compiled from edifying literature and philosophical writings. They were used in schools in the *progymnasmata*, the preliminary exercises in rhetoric, in which students reproduced and explained them in their own words and adapted them to different literary forms (43). Such gnomes were defined by rhetoricians as summary statements given in a general declaration to discourage or recommend something, or to explain the nature of each kind of action. A gnome was thought to differ from a chreia (41–43) in that the latter included a definite person, situation, and action. The last example from the *Gnomologium Vaticanum* (39), however, shows that the distinctions were not always observed by the persons who collected or used them. So too, while "Money is the root of all evil" (cf. 1 Tim 6:10) is clearly a gnome by the above rhetorical definition, Bion the Sophist said that "Love of money is the metropolis of evil" is a chreia (according to Theon, in L. Spengel, *Rhetores Graeci* [Leipzig: Teubner, 1854], 2.99,17). The gnomes could be collected and attributed to one philosopher (39) or associated with a philosophical school (40), but since they tended to represent what was useful rather than unique, individual gnomes were utilized in other forms of literature and attributed to different persons. Gnomes appear frequently in the Gospels, which illustrate the reasons for the common criticisms that the brevity of gnomes made them obscure (cf. Matt. 16:4), not as simple as they appeared (cf. Matt. 5:39), or impossible (cf. Matt. 5:29).

39

Gnomologium Vaticanum 459–464 (ed. Leo Sternbach [repr.; Berlin: Walter de Gruyter, 1963])

Pythagoras the philosopher advised that we should either remain silent or say something that is better than silence.

The same man said that we should flee the friendship of bad people and the hostility of good people.

The same man advised that we should choose the most excellent life, for habit would make it sweet.

The same man said that it was impossible to master a horse without a bridle or wealth without prudence.

The same man, when someone asked him how one might be rich, said, "If he is poor in pleasure."

Pythagoras, upon seeing an athletic young man putting on a lot of flesh by drinking wine, eating meat, and observing his diet, said, "O, my dear fellow, do stop making your prison so strong!"

40

The Pythagorean Sentences 14–29 (Henry Chadwick, *The Sentences of Sextus* [Cambridge: Cambridge University Press, 1959], 85–86)

It is not the wise man's tongue that is chiefly valued by God, but his deeds. Indeed, it is by remaining silent that the wise man honors God.

A garrulous and ignorant man dishonors God when he prays and offers sacrifices. The wise man alone is a priest, alone is dear to the gods, and alone knows how to pray.

Knowledge of God produces a man of few words.

The wise man, since he has been sent out naked, while naked will call to the one who sent him. For God will only listen to the person who is not encumbered by alien coverings.

Know that the character which can perfectly blend with you while you engage in philosophy is extremely rare.

One can receive no greater gift from God than virtue.

Votive gifts and sacrifices do not honor God; offerings are not an honor to God. But the inspired mind which is completely secure meets God, for like must come to like.

It is harder to serve the passions than tyrants.

It is better to talk to oneself than to one's neighbors.

The person who is in bondage to the passions and is controlled by them cannot be free.

Gentleness is a gift of the intelligence.

If someone honors God as though God needed his homage, he unconsciously considers himself to be greater than God.

If you always remember that wherever your body and soul perform an act God stands as your guardian, in all your deliberations and actions you will stand in constant awareness of the observer, and you will have God as your associate.

If you never fail to keep God in mind and believe that he watches over all things, because of your reverence for him he will protect you from all failure in your words and deeds.

As long as you are ignorant consider yourself mad.

A man must seek children who will remain behind after his release from this life.

It is better to live and be confident while lying on a mattress than to be agitated while owning a golden bed.

CHREIAI

Chreiai were used in much the same ways as gnomes (**39**). A chreia is an instructive anecdote or saying, and, like the gnome, is frequently found in the Gospels. It was defined by rhetoricians as referring to a particular person; it is not always general in nature, does not always give a moral lesson, and is not always simply a saying. An example of a chreia describing an action might be, "Diogenes, seeing a boy misbehave, beat his paedagogue." Verbal chreiai can be divided into the declarative and the responsive. The declarative chreia is frequently introduced by such a formula as, "Once when he observed that . . ." (cf. Luke 6:5, according to Codex Bezae, an ancient manuscript, "On the same day, seeing someone working on the sabbath, he said to him, 'Man, if indeed you know what you are doing, you are blessed; but if you do not know, you are cursed and a transgressor of the law.' ") The responsive chreia is introduced by, "When he was asked by . . ." (cf. Luke 12:13–14; 17:20–21). While the chreia differs from the gnome by including a definite person, situation, and action, the information on the setting only provides the framework for the saying, which contains the entire point of the chreia. The chreia might be followed by a statement explaining the principle incorporated in the chreia itself (cf. Luke 21:1–4, with the reason or principle in v. 4). The chreia was not always clearly distinguished from the apophthegm, a more general term describing the sayings of notable men. The following examples of the chreia on washing lettuce show how a chreia might be adapted, and how it was used in different types of literature.

41 Diogenes Laertius used the chreia in his biographies of the philosophers. Details as to the setting and dialogue partners change, but the point of the chreia, to contrast the ascetic Cynic and hedonistic lives, remains the same. Diogenes and Metrocles represent the former, Plato, Aristippus, and Theodorus the latter. Dionysius (fourth century B.C.) was ruler of Syracuse, where he played host to a number of philosophers, who, in the philosophic tradition, became associated with the luxurious life.

41a. Diogenes Laertius, *Lives of Eminent Philosophers* 6.58

Some authors affirm that the following also belongs to [Diogenes]: that Plato saw him washing lettuces, came up to him and quietly said to him, "Had you paid court to Dionysius, you wouldn't now be washing lettuces," and that he with equal calmness made answer, "If you had washed lettuces, you wouldn't have paid court to Dionysius."

41b. Diogenes Laertius, *Lives of Eminent Philosophers* 2.68

Diogenes, washing the dirt from his vegetables, saw [Aristippus] passing and jeered at him in these terms, "If you had learnt to make these your diet, you would not have paid court to kings," to which his rejoinder was, "And if you knew how to associate with men, you would not be washing vegetables."

41c. Diogenes Laertius, *Lives of Eminent Philosophers* 2.102

[Theodorus] is said on one occasion in Corinth to have walked abroad with a numerous train of pupils, and Metrocles the Cynic, who was washing chervil, remarked, "You, sophist that you are, would not have wanted all these pupils if you had washed vegetables." Thereupon Theodorus retorted, "And you, if you had known how to associate with men, would have had no use for these vegetables."

42 Horace incorporated the chreia in a real letter to support an argument in favor of a moderate way of life.

Horace, *Epistle* 1.17.1–32

Even though, Scaeva, you look after your own interests quite wisely by yourself, though you know, on what terms, in fine, one should handle greater folk, yet learn the views of your humble friend, who still needs some teaching. It is as if a blind man sought to show the way; yet see whether even I have aught to say, which you may care to make your own.

If pleasant ease and sleep till sunrise be your delight, if dust and noise and wheels, or if tavern offend you, I shall order you off to Ferentinum. For joys fall not to the rich alone, and he has not lived amiss who from birth to death has passed unknown. But if you wish to help your friends and to treat yourself a little more generously, you in your hunger will make for a rich table.

"If Aristippus could be content to dine on greens, he would not want to live with princes." "If he who censures me knew how to live with princes, he would sniff at greens." Of these two sages tell me whose words and deeds you approve; or, since you are the younger, hear why the view of Aristippus is the better. For this is the way, as the story goes, that he dodged the snapping Cynic: "I play the buffoon for my own profit, you for the people's. My conduct is better and nobler by far. I do service that I may have a horse to ride and be fed by a prince: you sue for paltry doles; but you become inferior to the giver, though you pose as needing no man." To Aristippus every form of life was fitting, every condition and circumstance; he aimed at higher things, but as a rule was content with what he had. On the other hand, take the man whom endurance clothes with its double rags: I shall marvel if a changed mode of life befit him. The one will not wait for a purple mantle; he will put on anything and walk through the most crowded streets, and in no inelegant fashion will play either part. The other will shun a cloak woven

at Miletus as worse than a dog or a snake, and will die of cold
if you do not give him back his rags. Give them back and let
him live his uncouth life.

43 In the fictitious letter of Pseudo-Diogenes, which was possibly
written as an exercise in style, the chreia became the occasion
of the letter itself.

Pseudo-Diogenes, *Epistle* 32

To Aristippus, greeting. I learned that you have devoted
yourself to slandering me and to reproaching my poverty at
every opportunity you have before the tyrant, saying that
you once caught me at the well washing off chicory as an
appetizer for my bread. But I am amazed, my fine friend, at
how you abuse the poverty of those who commend worthy
practices, especially since you have heard and followed the
same recommendations from Socrates, who wore the same
coarse cloak winter, summer and at all other times. He held
the same common rights to be applicable to his wives and
did not get his appetizers from the gardens or kitchens, but
from the gymnasia. But you seem to have forgotten these
facts because of the Sicilian banquets.

But I will not remind you how much poverty is valued,
especially at Athens, nor shall I defend myself for it (for in
my case I do not impart my own good to you, as you give
your goods to others. So it is enough for me that I alone
know for certain about it). But I shall remind you a bit about
Dionysius and his blessed company, which delights you. I
mean the occasions when you are eating and drinking at
extravagant dinners, the likes of which would never be held
in my presence, when you see some men being whipped,
others fixed to the stake. others driven to the stone quarries,
and the wives of some taken away for wanton purposes, as
are the children of others, and many of the slaves, not just
of one man or of the ruler himself, but of many unholy men.
And when you see someone forced to drink, lingering, then
going his way, but unable to flee because of his golden
shackles.

I, for one, remind you of these things in return for those
reproaches. How much better do we live, who know how to
wash chicory but do not know how to dance attendance at
the doors of Dionysius! I declare, we live better than you

who advise Dionysius ana give orders o all of Sicily. But however much you rail against us in your extreme boldness, you should have sense, nor should reason rise up against the passions. For the things in Dionysius' court are fine according to all reports, but the freedom in the time of Chronos . . .

POETRY

Compilations of quotations from the poets were made to be easily memorized and were used extensively in schools. On the primary level, children were given maxims extracted from the poets to copy as writing exercises and memorize. The quotations from the poets quickly became proverbial, and, since their inclusion in anthologies made them common property, it is not always possible to determine whether an author who quoted or used them was aware of their ultimate origin (cf. Euripides: Acts 5:39; 26:14; Epimenides: Titus 1:12). As students progressed through the curriculum, they studied the full texts of the poets for their moral value, and still later analyzed them for their poetic quality and style.

Schoolchildren began their study of the poets themselves with the epics of Homer and Virgil, then proceeded to the tragedians Aeschylus, Sophocles, and Euripides. While tragedy and epic provided obvious serious lessons on human conduct, careful thought was given to when comedy should be introduced, for it contained much of a lower moral tone. Of the comics, Menander was the favorite (cf. 1 Cor. 15:33), and maxims from his and Euripides' works were popular as copying exercises on the primary level, but the reading of his plays was reserved for a later stage in the curriculum.

44 Plutarch provides an example of a moralizing interpretation of Homer and of the view that poetry is an appropriate introduction to philosophy for the young, but elsewhere he cautions that youngsters need guides to instruct them in interpreting morally ambiguous passages.

Plutarch, *How to Study Poetry* 15E–16A

So let us not root up or destroy the Muses' vine of poetry, but where the mythical and dramatic part grows all riotous and luxuriant, through pleasure unalloyed, which gives it boldness and obstinacy in seeking acclaim, let us take it in hand and prune it and pinch it back. But where with its grace

it approaches a true kind of culture, and the sweet allure-
ment of its language is not fruitless or vacuous, there let us
introduce philosophy and blend it with poetry. For as the
mandragora, when it grows beside the vine and imparts its
influence to the wine, makes this weigh less heavily on those
who drink it, so poetry, by taking up its themes from philosophy and blending them with fable, renders the task of learning light and agreeable for the young. Wherefore poetry
should not be avoided by those who are intending to pursue
philosophy, but they should use poetry as an introductory
exercise in philosophy, by training themselves habitually to
seek the profitable in what gives pleasure, and to find satis-
faction therein; and if there be nothing profitable, to combat
such poetry and be dissatisfied with it. For this is the beginning of education, "If one begin each task in proper way, so
is it likely will the ending be" [Nauck, *T.G.E.*, *Sophocles* 747],
as Sophocles says.

45   Dio Chrysostom shows the value of the poets to a philosophical preacher to the masses (cf. Acts 17:28). They generally
have a reputation for wisdom and represent the values of the
majority of people. For that very reason, however, although
the philosopher might use the poets in his teaching, he does
not do so uncritically **(44)**.

Dio Chrysostom, *Oration* **7.97–102**

Is it not, then, most unfitting to admire wealth as the poet
[Euripides, *Electra* 404f.?] does and regard it as really worth
seeking? He says that its greatest good lies in giving to
guests and, when any who are used to luxury come to one's
house, being in a position to offer them lodging and set such
tokens of hospitality before them as would please them
most. And in advancing these views we cite the poets, not to
gainsay them idly nor because we are envious of the reputation for wisdom that they have won by their poems; no, it is
not for these reasons we covet the honour of showing them
to be wrong, but because we think that it is in them especially
that we shall find the thought and feeling of men generally,
just what the many think about wealth and the other objects
of their admiration, and what they consider would be the
greatest good derived from each of them. For it is evident
that men would not love the poets so passionately nor extol

them as wise and good and exponents of the truth if the
poetry did not echo their own sentiments nor express their
own views. Since, then, it is not possible to take each member of the multitude aside and show him his error or to
cross-question everybody in turn by saying, "How is it, sir,
that you fear poverty so exceedingly and exalt riches so
highly?" and again, "What great profit do you expect to win
if you happen to have amassed wealth or, let us say, to have
turned merchant or even become a king?" Such a procedure
would involve infinite trouble and is altogether impractica-
ble. Therefore, because we must, let us go to their prophets
and spokesmen, the poets, with the conviction that we shall
find among them the beliefs of the many clearly put and
enshrined in verse; and in truth I do not think that we fall
very far short of our object in so doing. And our present
procedure, I believe, is the usual one even with men wiser
than myself.

THE USE OF PHILOSOPHIC COMPILATIONS

Possibly as early as at the end of secondary education, in introductory studies in philosophy, compilations of gnomes (gnomologies)
(**39, 40**) and chreiai, summaries of a philosopher's thought (**37**), and
handbooks (**36, 60**) might be used. Compilations were also widely
used outside the classroom. Seneca made compilations for his own
personal use but was conscious of their value for others (*Epistle* 84).
Plutarch (**38**), in making his collection on the married life for his
young friends, was following common practice. Serious philosophers, however, did not make or use such compilations without
reservation.

46 Pseudo-Plutarch illustrates the use made in schools of a collection of obscure statements by Pythagoras. The "allegories"
require explanation and are the type of material to engage
students in their early teens. Although the author introduces
the Pythagorean collection to support his admonition that the
young should not associate with base men, they do not all deal
with that particular matter.

Pseudo-Plutarch, *The Education of Children* 12D–F

It should be the general rule to keep the young away from
any association with base men; for they carry away some-

thing of their badness. This duty Pythagoras also has enjoined in the form of allegories which I shall now quote and
explain. For they contribute no small influence towards the
acquisition of virtue. For example: "Do not taste of black-
tails"; that is, "Do not spend your time with men of black
character, because of their malevolence." "Do not step over
the beam of a balance"; that is, one should give greatest
heed to justice and not transgress it. "Do not sit on a peck
measure"; as much as to say that we should avoid idleness
and have forethought for providing our daily bread. "Do not
give your hand to everybody"; instead of, "Do not make
friends too readily." "Do not wear a tight ring"; means that
one should live his life unhampered, and not subject it to any
bond. "Do not poke a fire with steel," instead of, "Do not
provoke an angry man." Indeed, it is wrong to do so, and we
should yield to men who are in a temper. "Do not eat your
heart"; as much as to say, "Do not injure your soul by wast-
ing it with worries." "Abstain from beans"; means that a
man should keep out of politics, for beans were used in
earlier times for voting upon the removal of magistrates
from office. "Do not put food into a slop-pail"; signifies that
it is not fitting to put clever speech into a base mind. For
speech is the food of thought, and baseness in men makes
it unclean. "Do not turn back on reaching the boundaries";
that is, when people are about to die and see the boundary
of their life close at hand, they should bear all this with
serenity and not be faint-hearted.

47 Seneca warns against becoming dependent on compilations.
The person making moral progress should move beyond the
memorization of school exercises to develop, from his own
experience, his own maxims.

Seneca, *Epistle* **33.5–9**

For this reason, give over hoping that you can skim, by
means of epitomes, the wisdom of distinguished men. Look
into their wisdom as a whole; study it as a whole. They are
working out a plan and weaving together, line upon line, a
masterpiece, from which nothing can be taken away without
injury to the whole. Examine the separate parts, if you like,
provided you examine them as parts of the man himself. She

is not a beautiful woman whose ankle or arm is praised, but she whose general appearance makes you forget to admire her single attributes.

If you insist, however, I shall not be niggardly with you, but lavish; for there is a huge multitude of these passages; they are scattered about in profusion,—they do not need to be gathered together, but merely to be picked up. They do not drip forth occasionally; they flow continuously. They are unbroken and are closely connected. Doubtless they would be of much benefit to those who are still novices and worshipping outside the shrine; for the single maxims sink in more easily when they are marked off and bounded like a line of verse. That is why we give to children a proverb, or that which the Greeks call *Chria,* to be learned by heart; that sort of thing can be comprehended by the young mind, which cannot as yet hold more. For a man, however, whose progress is definite, to chase after choice extracts and to prop his weakness by the best known and the briefest sayings and to depend upon his memory, is disgraceful; it is time for him to lean on himself. He should make such maxims and not memorize them. For it is disgraceful even for an old man, or one who has sighted old age, to have a note-book knowledge. "This is what Zeno [founder of Stoicism, fourth to third century B.C.] said." But what have you yourself said? "This is the opinion of Cleanthes [Stoic philosopher]." But what is your own opinion? How long shall you march under another man's orders? Take command, and utter some word which posterity will remember. Put forth something from your own stock. For this reason I hold that there is nothing of eminence in all such men as these, who never create anything themselves, but always lurk in the shadow of others, playing the role of interpreters, never daring to put once into practice what they have been so long in learning. They have exercised their memories on other men's material. But it is one thing to remember, another to know. Remembering is merely safeguarding something entrusted to the memory; knowing, however, means making everything your own; it means not depending upon the copy and not all the time glancing back at the master. "Thus said Zeno, thus said Cleanthes, indeed!" Let there be a difference between yourself and your book! How long shall you be a learner? From now on be a teacher as well! "But why," one asks, "should

I have to continue hearing lectures on what I can read?"
"The living voice," one replies, "is a great help." Perhaps,
but not the voice which merely makes itself the mouthpiece
of another's words, and only performs the duty of a reporter.

48   Despite his reservations, Seneca still used maxims because
they expressed universal sentiments, whether they were
derived from Stoics, Epicureans, or some unknown comic
poet. His use of compilations is reflected in his custom of
deliberately including at least one maxim from them in each of
his letters.

Seneca, *Epistle* 9.19–21

We marvel at certain animals because they can pass through
fire and suffer no bodily harm; but how much more marvellous is a man who has marched forth unhurt and unscathed
through fire and sword and devastation! Do you understand
now how much easier it is to conquer a whole tribe than to
conquer one *man?* This saying of Stilbo [philosopher of the
Megarian school, fourth century B.C.] makes common
ground with Stoicism; the Stoic also can carry his goods
unimpaired through cities that have been burned to ashes;
for he is self-sufficient. Such are the bounds which he sets to
his own happiness.

But you must not think that our school alone can utter
noble words; Epicurus himself, the reviler of Stilbo, spoke
similar language; put it down to my credit, though I have
already wiped out my debt for the present day. He says:
"Whoever does not regard what he has as most ample
wealth, is unhappy, though he be master of the whole
world." Or, if the following seems to you a more suitable
phrase,—for we must try to render the meaning and not the
mere words: "A man may rule the world and still be unhappy, if he does not feel that he is supremely happy." In
order, however, that you may know that these sentiments are
universal, suggested, of course, by Nature, you will find in
one of the comic poets this verse: "Unblest is he who thinks
himself unblest."

5

Styles of Exhortation

Moral philosophers constantly distinguished themselves from professional orators. Their aim was to move people to action by exposing their moral condition, holding out the promises of a rational life, and persuading them to decide for the good (22, 23). The speech in which they attempted to accomplish this could be harsh or gentle, biting or soothing, but it was always to be frank and aim at the benefit of the hearer. Speeches of the orators, the moralists charged, drew attention either to the speeches or the speakers themselves or were vain because they strove to please rather than benefit (1). That some of the philosophers claimed to avoid the rhetorical style of display (epideictic) does not mean, however, that they did not reflect on the nature of speech or develop styles peculiarly suited to their aims (17, 29, 30). The responsible teacher who adapted himself to the conditions of his hearers knew a wide range of styles of persuasion and was sensitive to how appropriate or inappropriate they were to any particular circumstance (20, 21). The following three modes of exhortation are related by the practicality of their aims, their unadorned language, and the devices they use. Modern distinctions between them are sometimes sharper than ancient practice justifies. While it is true, for example, that Clement of Alexandria differentiated between protrepsis and paraenesis (*Paedagogue* 1.1), the terms had been used interchangeably before him and continued to be used so after him. Thus Pseudo-Justin (third century) calls his protrepsis a *Paraenetic Address to the Greeks*, and Ennodius (fifth century), in his *Paraenesis didascalia*, in which he praises rhetoric as the most important branch of learning and a fit guide to higher education, makes his appeal in the manner of a protrepsis. More important than the nomenclature attached to them are their aims and the ways in which they sought to attain them.

PROTREPSIS

Protrepsis is designed to win someone over to a particular enterprise or way of life by demonstrating its superiority. First practiced by orators in the political arena and the law courts, it had become popular by the middle of the third century B.C. when the young Aristotle, in reaction to Isocrates, wrote his *Protrepticus,* which was an eloquent invitation to the philosophic life. Although preserved only in fragments, it appears to have contained a systematic argument in favor of philosophy. A follower of Isocrates replied to Aristotle in *To Demonicus* **(50)** which redressed the balance by stressing the practical over the contemplative life. Protrepsis then continued to enlist recruits for the philosophic enterprise itself or for the moral life grounded in and guided by philosophy **(6, 7, 31)**.

In Christian literature, it makes its appearance in the second century in different literary forms: letters (e.g., *Epistle to Diognetus, Letter of Ptolemy to Flora*), epideictic discourses (e.g., Clement of Alexandria, *Protrepticus*), Socratic dialogues (e.g., Minucius Felix), and in defenses of Christianity.

49 In this discourse Epictetus opposes his fictive dialogue partner who defends the philosopher's use of epideictic oratory, that is, the style of exhibition or display. Epictetus admits the appropriateness of praising some speeches but insists that the philosopher's, which reveals moral illness and causes pain, is neither designed to give nor cause pleasure which results in praise of the speaker. Rather than epideixis, protrepsis is the philosopher's proper mode of exhortation. Together with refutation or reproof, which exposes the human condition (cf. Titus 1:9, 13; 2:15; Hermas, *Vis.* 1.1.5), and teaching, protrepsis does not make an oratorical display but reveals the inner inconsistency in the philosopher's hearers and brings them to conversion **(22, 23, 57)**.

Epictetus, *Discourse* **3.23.23–38**

Why should I listen to you? Do you want to exhibit to me the clever way in which you put words together? You do compose them cleverly, man; and what good is it to you? "But praise me." What do you mean by "praise"? "Cry out to me, 'Bravo!' or 'Marvellous!' " All right, I'll say it. But if praise is some one of those things which the philosophers put in the category of the good, what praise can I give you? If it is a good thing to speak correctly, teach me and I will praise you. What then? Ought one to take no pleasure in listening to such efforts? Far from it. I do not fail to take pleasure in listening to a citharoede [someone who performs on the cithara]; surely I am not bound for that reason to stand and sing to my own accompaniment on the harp, am I? Listen, what does Socrates say? "Nor would it be seemly for me, O men of Athens, at my time of life to appear before you like some lad, and weave a cunning discourse" [Plato, *Apology* 17C]. "Like some lad," he says. For it is indeed a dainty thing, this small art of selecting trivial phrases and putting them together, and of coming forward and reading or reciting them gracefully, and then in the midst of delivery shouting out, "There are not many people who can follow this, by your lives, I swear it!"

Does a philosopher invite people to a lecture?—Is it not rather the case that, as the sun draws its own sustenance to itself, so he also draws to himself those to whom he is to do good? What physician ever invites a patient to come and be healed by him? Although I am told that in these days the physicians in Rome *do* advertise; however, in my time they were called in by their patients. "I invite you to come and hear that you are in a bad way, and that you are concerned with anything rather than what you should be concerned with, and that you are ignorant of the good and the evil, and are wretched and miserable." That's a fine invitation! And yet if the philosopher's discourse does not produce this effect, it is lifeless and so is the speaker himself. Rufus used to say, "If you have nothing better to do than to praise me, then I am speaking to no purpose." Wherefore he spoke in such a way that each of us as we sat there fancied someone had gone to Rufus and told him of our faults; so effective was his grasp of what men actually do, so vividly did he set before each man's eyes his particular weaknesses.

Men, the lecture-room of the philosopher is a hospital; you ought not to walk out of it in pleasure, but in pain. For you are not well when you come; one man has a dislocated shoulder, another an abscess, another a fistula, another a headache. And then am I to sit down and recite to you dainty little notions and clever little mottoes, so that you will go out with words of praise on your lips, one man carrying away his shoulder just as it was when he came in, another his head in the same state, another his fistula, another his abscess? And so it's for this, is it, that young men are to travel from home, and leave their parents, their friends, their relatives, and their bit of property, merely to cry "Bravo!" as you recite your clever little mottoes? Was this what Socrates used to do, or Zeno, or Cleanthes?

Well! But isn't there such a thing as the right style for exhortation [*protrepsis*]?—Why yes, who denies that? Just as there is the style for refutation, and the style for instruction. Who, then, has ever mentioned a fourth style along with these, the style of display? Why, what *is* the style of exhortation? The ability to show to the individual, as well as to the crowd, the warring inconsistency in which they are floundering about, and how they are paying attention to anything rather than what they truly want. For they want the things that conduce to happiness, but they are looking for them in the wrong place. To achieve that must a thousand benches be placed, and the prospective audience be invited, and you put on a fancy cloak, or dainty mantle, and mount the speaker's stand, and paint a word-picture of—how Achilles died? By the gods, I beseech you, have done with discrediting, as far as it is in your power to discredit, words and actions that are noble! There is nothing more effective in the style for exhortation than when the speaker makes clear to his audience that he has need of them. Or tell me, who that ever heard you reading a lecture or conducting a discourse felt greatly disturbed about himself, or came to a realization of the state he was in, or on going out said, "The philosopher brought it home to me in fine style; I must not act like this any longer"? But doesn't he say to a companion, if you make an unusually fine impression, "That was beautiful diction in the passage about Xerxes"; and doesn't the other answer, "No, I preferred the one about the battle of Thermopylae"? Is this what listening to a philosopher amounts to?

PARAENESIS

Paraenesis is moral exhortation in which someone is advised to pursue or abstain from something. It appears in many forms of communication, especially speeches, letters (cf. 1 Peter 2:11–5:11; *1 Clem.* 4–39; *Barn.* 18–20), and tractates which may assume some epistolary features (cf. Heb. 13:1–19; James). Paraenesis is broader in scope than protrepsis; it contains useful rules for conduct in common situations and adopts styles that range from censure to consolation.

Modern scholars have focused on the formal characteristics of paraenesis. That its content is traditional and not new is indicated by such phrases as "as you know" (cf. 1 Thess. 1:5; 2:2, 5, 11; 3:4). Related to this feature is its general applicability, which does not mean, however, that paraenesis is not related or adapted to the settings in which it is given (27). Since what is advised is already known (67), the exhorter disavows the need for further instruction (cf. 2 Cor. 9:1; 1 Thess. 4:9; 5:1), but merely reminds his listeners of what they already know (cf. 1 Thess. 2:9; 3:6). He similarly compliments them for what they are already doing (cf. 1 Thess. 4:1, 10; 5:11; Ignatius, *Pol.* 1.2; *Eph.* 4.1; *Trall.* 2.2), and encourages them to continue (cf. 1 Thess. 4:1, 10). To provide concreteness to the exhortation, an example is offered for imitation (see pp. 135–138; cf. Acts 20:31–34; 1 Thess. 1:6; 2 Thess. 3:7–9). The example is frequently delineated antithetically (cf. 1 Thess. 2:1–8) and often is a member of the family, particularly one's father (cf. 1 Cor. 4:14–17). Paraenetic advice may be diverse in content and consist of brief admonitions strung together (cf. Romans 12; 13; James 1), or it may be more expanded in form (cf. James 2; 3; Hermas, *Mandates*).

50   The classic example of paraenesis ascribed to Isocrates exhibits these features as well as the use of other conventions, for example, lists of duties.

Pseudo-Isocrates, *To Demonicus* 9–15

Nay, if you will but recall your father's principles, you will have from your own house a noble illustration of what I am telling you. For he did not belittle virtue nor pass his life in indolence; on the contrary, he trained his body by toil, and by his spirit he withstood dangers. Nor did he love wealth inordinately; but, though he enjoyed the good things at his hand as became a mortal, yet he cared for his possessions as if he had been immortal. Neither did he order his existence sordidly, but was a lover of beauty, munificent in his manner of life, and generous to his friends; and he prized more those who were devoted to him than those who were his kin by blood; for he considered that in the matter of companionship nature is a much better guide than convention, character than kinship, and freedom of choice than compulsion.

But all time would fail us if we should try to recount all his activities. On another occasion I shall set them forth in detail; for the present, however, I have produced a sample of the nature of Hipponicus, after whom you should pattern your life as after an ensample, regarding his conduct as your law, and striving to imitate and emulate your father's virtue; for it were a shame, when painters represent the beautiful among animals, for children not to imitate the noble among their ancestors. Nay, you must consider that no athlete is so in duty bound to train against his competitors as are you to take thought how you may vie with your father in his ways of life. It is not possible for the mind to be so disposed unless one is fraught with many maxims; for, as it is the nature of the body to be developed by appropriate exercises, it is the nature of the soul to be developed by moral precepts. Wherefore I shall endeavour to set before you concisely by what practices I think you can make the most progress toward virtue and win the highest repute in the eyes of all other men.

First of all, then, show devotion to the gods, not merely by doing sacrifice, but also by keeping your vows; for the former is but evidence of a material prosperity, whereas the latter is proof of a noble character. Do honour to the divine power at all times, but especially on occasions of public worship; for thus you will have the reputation both of sacrificing to the gods and of abiding by the laws.

Conduct yourself toward your parents as you would have your children conduct themselves toward you.

Train your body, not by the exercises which conduce to strength, but by those which conduce to health. In this you will succeed if you cease your exertions while you still have energy to exert yourself.

Be not fond of violent mirth, nor harbour presumption of speech; for the one is folly, the other madness.

Whatever is shameful to do you must not consider it honourable even to mention. Accustom yourself to be, not of a stern, but of a thoughtful, mien; for through the former you will be thought self-willed, through the latter, intelligent. Consider that no adornment so becomes you as modesty, justice, and self-control; for these are the virtues by which, as all men are agreed, the character of the young is held in restraint.

51 Seneca, by engaging in the debate over the use of paraenesis, provides some of the reasoning that either is behind paraenesis or justifies it.

Seneca, *Epistle* 94.1, 21, 25–26, 32–35, 39

1. That department of philosophy which supplies precepts appropriate to the individual case, instead of framing them for mankind at large—which, for instance, advises how a husband should conduct himself towards his wife, or how a father should bring up his children, or how a master should rule his slaves—this department of philosophy, I say, is accepted by some as the only significant part, while the other departments are rejected on the ground that they stray beyond the sphere of practical needs—as if any man could give advice concerning a portion of life without having first gained a knowledge of the sum of life as a whole!

21. "But," comes the reply, "error is the source of sin; precepts do not remove error, nor do they rout our false opinions on the subject of Good and Evil." I admit that precepts alone are not effective in overthrowing the mind's mistaken beliefs; but they do not on that account fail to be of service when they accompany other measures also. In the first place, they refresh the memory; in the second place, when sorted into their proper classes, the matters which showed themselves in a jumbled mass when considered as a whole, can be considered in this way with greater care. According to our opponents' theory, you might even say that consolation and exhortation were superfluous. Yet they are not superfluous; neither, therefore, is counsel.

25–26. People say: "What good does it do to point out the obvious?" A great deal of good; for we sometimes know facts without paying attention to them. Advice is not teaching; it merely engages the attention and rouses us, and concentrates the memory, and keeps it from losing grip. We miss much that is set before our very eyes. Advice is, in fact, a sort of exhortation. The mind often tries not to notice even that which lies before our eyes; we must therefore force upon it the knowledge of things that are perfectly well known. One might repeat here the saying of Calvus about Vatinius: "You all know that bribery has been going on, and everyone knows that you know it." You know that friendship should be scrupulously honoured, and yet you do not hold it in honour. You know that a man does wrong in requiring chastity of his wife while he himself is intriguing with the wives of other men; you know that, as your wife should have no dealings with a lover, neither should you yourself with a mistress; and yet you do not act accordingly. Hence, you must be continually brought to remember these facts; for they should not be in storage, but ready for use. And whatever is wholesome should be often discussed and often brought before the mind, so that it may be not only familiar to us, but also ready to hand. And remember, too, that in this way what is clear often becomes clearer.

32–35. Some say: "If one is familiar with upright and honourable dogmas, it will be superfluous to advise him." By no means; for this person has indeed learned to do things which he ought to do; but he does not see with sufficient clearness what these things are. For we are hindered from accomplishing praiseworthy deeds not only by our emotions, but also by want of practice in discovering the demands of a particular situation. Our minds are often under good control, and yet at the same time are inactive and untrained in finding the path of duty,–and advice makes this clear. Again, it is written: "Cast out all false opinions concerning Good and Evil, but replace them with true opinions; then advice will have no function to perform." Order in the soul can doubtless be established in this way; but these are not the only ways. For although we may infer by proofs just what Good and Evil are, nevertheless, precepts have their proper role. Prudence and justice consist of certain duties; and duties are set in order by precepts. Moreover, judgment as to Good and Evil is itself strengthened by following up our duties, and precepts conduct us to this end. For both are in accord with each other; nor can precepts take the lead unless the duties follow. They observe their natural order; hence precepts clearly come first.

"Precepts," it is said, "are numberless." Wrong again! For they are not numberless so far as concerns important and essential things. Of course there are slight distinctions, due to the time, or the place, or the person; but even in these cases, precepts are given which have a general application.

39. Furthermore, is not philosophy the Law of Life? Grant, if we will, that the laws do not avail; it does not necessarily follow that advice also should not avail. On this

ground, you ought to say that consolation does not avail, and warning, and exhortation, and scolding, and praising; since they are all varieties of advice. It is by such methods that we arrive at a perfect condition of mind.

DIATRIBE

Modern descriptions of the diatribe as literary genre, style, or simply popular philosophical literature show the difficulty of defining this mode of exhortation. The ancients only very rarely used the word to describe exhortation, but when they did, they had in mind the educational activity of teacher and student, not a literary genre. Modern scholars, however, have identified common elements of style, content, tone, and purpose in a sufficiently large number of sources to justify their classification of a particular type of exhortation which may more usefully, if not precisely, be described as a mode rather than a genre. Perhaps originated by Bion of Borysthenes (fourth to third century B.C.), but given its characteristic features by Teles (third to second century B.C.), the diatribe underwent changes as it was adopted by speakers and writers of different persuasion and adapted to their own circumstances. The diatribe is essentially a popular philosophical treatment of an ethical topic and has the practical aim of moving people to action rather than reflection. It is thus addressed to laymen rather than to specialists. The earlier diatribes (e.g., those of Teles) seem to have been lively, even entertaining, with a pronounced use of a dialogue with a fictive opponent lending spice to the whole. The later diatribes (e.g., those of Musonius, Seneca, Dio Chrysostom, Plutarch) are calmer in tone, more didactic, are arranged more systematically, and, while they retain the dialogical feature characteristic of the diatribe, are more restrained in using it. The diatribe could be used in different types of communication—for example, in letters (e.g., Seneca, Paul, James) as well as in discourses to the public (e.g., Dio Chrysostom, Plutarch, Maximus of Tyre) and instruction in school (e.g., Teles, Epictetus), and could be used to attain protreptic and paraenetic ends. It is to be expected that the personality of the speaker or author as well as his setting would affect the way in which he used this mode of persuasion.

The dialogical feature of the diatribe, which combines elements of the philosophical dialogue and satire, makes it vivid and lively. The interlocutor's question, frequently introduced by "Someone will say" (cf. 1 Cor. 15:35; see also Rom. 9:19; James 2:18) or anticipated by the speaker in his words (cf. Rom. 4:1; 6:1), could be answered by counterquestions to wear the opponent down (cf. Rom. 9:19–24) or by a response that highlights the absurdity of the objection (cf. 1 Cor. 15:35), although at times it does receive a serious reply containing an authoritative quotation (cf. Rom. 3:1–8). Impatience with the hearer is expressed in exclamations of "Fool!" (cf. 1 Cor. 15:36), "O man!" (cf. Rom. 2:1, 3; 9:20), and the like, and by ironic wishes (cf. 1 Cor. 4:8; 2 Cor. 11:1; Gal. 5:12). The syntax is always simple, with short, parallel sentences—for example, questions followed by a series of short answers (cf. 1 Cor. 3:5–9), parallel formulations (cf. Rom. 12:6–8), a series of negative sentences (cf. 1 Cor. 9:1), short rhetorical questions (Rom. 2:21–23; 1 Cor. 12:29–30), or parallelism with word plays and antitheses (cf. 1 Cor. 7:29–31; 9:19–22). The diatribe is peppered with rhetorical questions, frequently used for emphasis (cf. 1 Cor. 4:7; 9:4–6; James 2:14–16, 20–21) or to point to a common assumption (cf. 1 Cor. 6:2), which is also done by such introductory statements as, "Do you not know?" (cf. Rom. 6:16; 1 Cor. 3:16; 6:15; 9:24) and the use of sententious statements (cf. Rom. 14:7; 1 Cor. 5:6) or quotations from the poets (cf. 1 Cor. 15:33). Among the literary and rhetorical conventions, lists of vices and virtues (see pp. 138–141; cf. Rom. 1:29–31; 1 Cor. 6:9–10) and hardships (see pp. 141–143; cf. 2 Cor. 4:8–9; 6:9–10), the latter heavily loaded with paradox, are especially popular.

52 The diatribes of Epictetus (cf. **10, 49, 59**), which are not representative of his period but share much with the earlier diatribes, contain many of these features. So do the letters of Paul, particularly in their paraenetic and didactic sections, in which the dialogue serves to advance the argument.

Epictetus, *Discourse* 1.6.1–17

From everything that happens in the universe it is easy fo a man to find occasion to praise providence, if he has within himself these two qualities: the faculty of taking a comprehensive view of what has happened in each individual instance, and the sense of gratitude. Otherwise, one man will not see the usefulness of what has happened, and another, even if he does see it, will not be grateful therefor. If God had made colours, but had not made the faculty of seeing them, of what good had it been?—None at all.—But, conversely, if He had made the faculty, but in making objects, had made them incapable of falling under the faculty of vision, in that case also of what good had it been?—None at all.—What then, if He had even made both of these, but had not made light?—Even thus it would have been of no use. —Who is it, then, that has fitted this to that and that to this? And who is it that has fitted the sword to the scabbard, and the scabbard to the sword? No one? Assuredly from the very structure of all made objects we are accustomed to prove that the work is certainly the product of some artificer, and has not been constructed at random.

Does, then, every such work reveal its artificer, but do visible objects and vision and light not reveal him? And the male and the female, and the passion of each for intercourse with the other, and the faculty which makes use of the organs which have been constructed for this purpose, do these things not reveal their artificer either? Well, admit it for these things; but the marvellous constitution of the intellect, whereby, when we meet with sensible objects, we do not merely have their forms impressed upon us, but also make a selection from them, and subtract and add, and make these various combinations by using them, yes, and, by Zeus, pass from some things to certain others which are in a manner related to them—is not even all this sufficient to stir our friends and induce them not to leave the artificer out of account? Else let them explain to us what it is that produces each of these results, or how it is possible that objects so wonderful and so workmanlike should come into being at random and spontaneously.

What then? Is it in the case of man alone that these things occur? You will, indeed, find many things in man only, things of which the rational animal had a peculiar need, but you will also find many possessed by us in common with the irrational animals. Do they also, then, understand what happens? No! for use is one thing, and understanding another. God had need of the animals in that they make use of external impressions, and of us in that we understand the use of external impressions. And so for them it is sufficient to eat and drink and rest and procreate, and whatever else of the things within their own province the animals severally do; while for us, to whom He has made the additional gift of the faculty of understanding, these things are no longer sufficient, but unless we act appropriately, and methodically, and in conformity each with his own nature and constitution, we shall no longer achieve our own ends. For of beings whose constitutions are different, the works and the ends are likewise different. So for the being whose constitution is adapted to use only, mere use is sufficient, but where a being has also the faculty of understanding the use, unless the principle of propriety be added, he will never attain his end.

53   The diatribes of Musonius Rufus (cf. **5, 6, 15, 65, 66**) represent those diatribes which are calmer in tone and more systematic in structure. Musonius frequently, as he does here, conducts his discussion in terms of the cardinal virtues.

Musonius Rufus, *Fragment 3 (That Women Too Should Study Philosophy)*

When someone asked him if women too should study philosophy, he began to discourse on the theme that they should, in somewhat the following manner. Women as well as men, he said, have received from the gods the gift of reason, which we use in our dealings with one another and by which we judge whether a thing is good or bad, right or wrong. Likewise the female has the same senses as the male; namely sight, hearing, smell, and the others. Also both have the same parts of the body, and one has nothing more than the other. Moreover, not men alone, but women too, have a natural inclination toward virtue and the capacity for acquiring it, and it is the nature of women no less than men to be pleased by good and just acts and to reject the opposite of these. If this is true, by what reasoning would it ever be appropriate for men to search out and and consider how they may lead good lives, which is exactly the study of philosophy, but inappropriate for women? Could it be that it is fitting for men to be good, but not for women? Let us examine in detail the qualities which are suitable for a woman who would lead a good life, for it will appear that each of them would accrue to her most readily from the study of philosophy.

In the first place, a woman must be a good housekeeper; that is a careful accountant of all that pertains to the welfare of her house and capable of directing the household slaves. It is my contention that these are the very qualities which would be present particularly in the woman who studies philosophy, since obviously each of them is a part of life, and philosophy is nothing other than knowledge about life, and the philosopher, as Socrates said, quoting Homer, is constantly engaged in investigating precisely this: "Whatsoever of good and of evil is wrought in thy halls" [Homer, *Odyssey* 4.392].

But above all a woman must be chaste and self-controlled; she must, I mean, be pure in respect of unlawful love, exercise restraint in other pleasures, not be a slave to desire, not be contentious, not lavish in expense, nor extravagant in dress. Such are the works of a virtuous woman, and to them I would add yet these: to control her temper, not to be overcome by grief, and to be superior to uncontrolled emotion of every kind. Now these are the things which the teachings of philosophy transmit, and the person who has learned them and practices them would seem to me to have become a well-ordered and seemly character, whether man or woman. Well, then, so much for self-control.

As for justice, would not the woman who studies philosophy be just, would she not be a blameless life-partner, would she not be a sympathetic help-mate, would she not be an untiring defender of husband and children, and would she not be entirely free of greed and arrogance? And who better than the woman trained in philosophy—and she certainly of necessity if she has really acquired philosophy—would be disposed to look upon doing a wrong as worse than suffering one (as much worse as it is the baser), and to regard being worsted as better than gaining an unjust advantage? Moreover, who better than she would love her children more than life itself? What woman would be more just than such a one?

Now as for courage, certainly it is to be expected that the educated woman will be more courageous than the uneducated, and one who has studied philosophy than the one who has not; and she will not therefore submit to anything shameful because of fear of death or unwillingness to face hardship, and she will not be intimidated by anyone because he is of noble birth, or powerful, or wealthy, no, not even if he be the tyrant of her city. For in fact she has schooled herself to be high-minded and to think of death not as an evil and life not as a good, and likewise not to shun hardship and never for a moment to seek ease and indolence. So it is that such a woman is likely to be energetic, strong to endure pain, prepared to nourish her children at her own breast, and to serve her husband with her own hands, and willing to do things which some would consider no better than slaves' work.

Would not such a woman be a great help to the man who married her, an ornament to her relatives, and a good example for all who know her? Yes, but I assure you, some will say, that women who associate with philosophers are bound to be arrogant for the most part and presumptuous, in that abandoning their own households and turning to the company of men they practice speeches, talk like sophists, and analyze syllogisms, when they ought to be sitting home spinning. I should not expect the women who study philosophy to shirk their appointed tasks for mere talk any more than men, but I maintain that their discussions should be conducted for the sake of their practical application. For as there is no merit in the science of medicine unless it conduces to the healing of man's body, so if a philosopher has or teaches reason, it is of no use if it does not contribute to the virtue of man's soul. Above all, we ought to examine the doctrine which we think women who study philosophy ought to follow; we ought to see if the study which presents modesty as the greatest good can make them presumptuous, if the study which is a guide to the greatest self-restraint accustoms them to live heedlessly, if what sets forth intemperance as the greatest evil does not teach self-control, if what represents the management of a household as a virtue does not impel them to manage well their homes. Finally, the teachings of philosophy exhort the woman to be content with her lot and to work with her own hands.

6
Literary and Rhetorical Conventions

In addition to numerous topoi (conventional subjects), the moralists made heavy use of certain minor literary and rhetorical conventions. One of these is the image of the Two Ways. The image of a man at a crossroads, challenged to choose between a life of virtue and one of vice, is found as early as Prodicus' (sophist, contemporary of Socrates) allegory of Heracles (Xenophon, *Memorabilia* 2. 1.21–33) and appears with great regularity in the moral literature (cf. Matt. 7:13–14; *Did.* 1–6; *Barn.* 18–20, all three of which, however, may have Jewish roots). The lists of duties of members of a household *(Haustafeln)* to the gods, the state, and various members within the household (**4, 50, 51**) reflect the tendency to reduce more extended discussions of common moral topics (**36, 60**) to lists which are evocative of such standard teaching. As important as the content of such lists were the functions they were made to perform in exhortations.

PERSONAL EXAMPLES

One of the most common devices used was the example. Insects (**61**), the heavenly bodies (**61**; cf. *1 Clem.* 20), and mythical figures (**31**) were all pressed into service as models of virtue. But personal examples in particular were used because they were regarded as more persuasive than words (**26**) and as providing concrete models to imitate (**50, 55, 56**; cf. Heb. 13:7; *1 Clem.* 17–18; 55; Polycarp, *Phil.* 8–9). It was therefore common to string together examples of individuals to illustrate virtues or vices (cf. Heb. 11:4–38; *1 Clem.* 9–12). A virtuous person was to offer an example (**53**; cf. 2 Thess. 3:6–13; 1 Tim. 4:11–12); a philosopher's practical example of the principles he taught (**26, 36g, 65**; cf. Acts 20:31–35; contrast Matt. 23:2–7) was thought to be a most important demonstration of his integrity. It was common, however, to refer to the example of other persons, especially to members of one's own family, one's father in particular (**50, 55;** cf. 1 Cor. 4:14–17; 2 Tim. 1:5), and to ancient worthies, while recognizing that contemporary models were also available (**25, 26, 54;** cf. 1 Peter 3:5–6; *1 Clem.* 4–5). Examples of vice were equally common (**56;** cf. 1 Cor. 10:1–13; 2 Tim. 3:8) and were frequently delineated, as were the patterns of virtue, by means of lists (**57;** cf. Phil. 4:8–9). Examples of both were carefully and widely used in protrepsis and paraenesis (**31, 50, 57;** cf. James 2:18–26; Jude 6–7). Antithesis is a common feature in the use of examples. An example could, for instance, be described antithetically (**50;** cf. 1 Thess. 2:1–8; 1 Peter 2:21–25), or a positive example could be balanced by or juxtaposed to a negative one (**31;** cf. 1 Corinthians 9; 10:1–13; 2 Tim. 2:1–9, 10–15; 2 Peter 2:4–8). Examples were used in many literary forms, from biographies (**56**) to letters (cf. *1 Clement*). They could also be presented implicitly in the form of autobiography (**17;** cf. 1 Thessalonians 1–3) or, more subtly, in letters written in the name of someone else who is thereby advanced as a model (**43;** cf. 2 Timothy).

54   Lucian begins his description of Demonax (second century A.D.), a Cynic of humane instincts, by reflecting on the use of contemporary models and juxtaposing him to Sostratus, the ascetic philosopher, whom he also admires.

Lucian, *Demonax* **1–2**

It was on the cards, it seems, that our modern world should not be altogether destitute of noteworthy and memorable men, but should produce enormous physical prowess and a highly philosophic mind. I speak with reference to the Boeotian Sostratus, whom the Greeks called Heracles and believed to be that hero, and especially to Demonax, the philosopher. Both these men I saw myself, and saw with wonderment: and under one of them, Demonax, I was long a student. I have written about Sostratus elsewhere, and have described his size and extraordinary strength, his open-air life on Parnassus, his bed that was no bed of ease, his mountain fare and his deeds (not inconsistent with his name) achieved in the way of slaying robbers, making roads in untravelled country and bridging places hard to pass. It is now fitting to tell of Demonax for two reasons—that he may be retained in memory by men of culture as far as I can bring it about, and that young men of good instincts who aspire to philosophy may not have to shape themselves by ancient precedents alone, but may be able to set themselves a pattern from our modern world and to copy that man, the best of all philosophers whom I know about.

55 Pliny emphasizes the value of a living personal model, particularly one's father, whom one may imitate.

Pliny, *Letter* 8.13

I much approve of your having read my orations with your father. It is important for your progress, to learn from a man of his eloquence what to admire and what to condemn, and by the same course of training to acquire the habit of speaking your real sentiments. You see whose steps you ought to follow; and happy are you in having a living model before you, which is at once the nearest and the noblest you can pursue! Happy, in a word, that he whom nature designed you should most resemble, is, of all others, the person whom you should most imitate! Farewell.

56 Plutarch's biographies were written partly to provide models for conduct. Here, after having discussed the power of the senses to distinguish between opposites, he justifies his inclusion of persons who were examples of inferior conduct.

Plutarch, *Demetrius* 1.4–6

Accordingly, the ancient Spartans would put compulsion upon their helots at the festivals to drink much unmixed wine, and would then bring them into the public messes, in order to show their young men what it was to be drunk. And though I do not think that the perverting of some to secure the setting right of others is very humane, or a good civil policy, still when men have led reckless lives, and have become conspicuous, in the exercise of power or in great undertakings, for badness, perhaps it will not be much amiss for me to introduce a pair or two of them into my biographies, though not that I may merely divert and amuse my readers by giving variety to my writing. Ismenias the Theban [a musician, fifth to fourth century B.C.] used to exhibit both good and bad players to his pupils on the flute and say, "you must play like this one," or again, "you must not play like this one"; and Antigenidas [musician and composer, fifth century B.C.) used to think that young men would listen with more pleasure to good flute players if they were given an experience of bad ones also. So, I think, we also shall be more eager to observe and imitate the better lives if we are not left without narratives of the blameworthy and the bad.

LISTS OF VIRTUES AND VICES

Catalogs of virtues and vices were used widely but not indiscriminately. In their content they tended to represent generally held views; nevertheless the presence or absence of certain items reflected the values of their authors. It is noteworthy, for example, that as common a pagan virtue as "humane" *(philanthropos)* appears so rarely in early Christian writings, and the Jewish and Christian "long-suffering" *(makrothymōs;* cf. Hermas, *Mand.* 5.1.1; 8.10) so rarely in pagan sources. The forms of the lists are varied, ranging from a simple list (e.g., Gal. 5:19–23), to a chain (e.g., 2 Peter 1:5–7), to a dialogue (e.g., Hermas, *Mand.* 2–5). The functions that the lists perform are similarly diverse. Basically, they were viewed as a device used in characterization (**57;** cf. Matt. 15: 19; 1 Tim. 1:8–10; James 3:13–18). As a supplement to precepts, they illustrated virtue and vice concretely and thus were useful in instruction (cf. Seneca, *Epistle* 95.65–67). As illustrations they were not all-inclusive but merely identified salient characteristics of the particular virtue or vice, and frequently concluded in an open-ended way (e.g., Rom. 1:31; Gal. 5:21, 23; 1 Tim. 1:10; Hermas, *Mand.* 8.10). When used paraenetically, virtues and vices could be used in antithesis (e.g., Gal. 5:19–23; Col. 3:5–17; James 3:13–18; 1 Peter 2:1–2; *1 Clem.* 13), remind the reader of an earlier worse condition (cf. 1 Cor. 6:9–11; Col. 3:12–13), or appear by themselves (e.g., 2 Peter 1:5–7; *1 Clem.* 3.5). The lists were effectively used in protreptic, the vices frequently listed first to depict tne diseased soul (**17, 20**) in moral slavery (**69**) from which philosophy would rescue it (**6**). Protrepsis, like paraenesis, therefore used lists to describe the contrast between the two lives (**58;** cf. **22, 31, 49;** cf. Col. 3:7; Titus 3:1–7). Vice lists could obviously be used polemically (e.g., 1 Tim. 1:9–10; 6:3–5; 2 Tim. 3:2–5) and also to assert the sage's superiority by claiming his victory over vice (**11**). As wise man the ideal king would embody all virtues, and the lists are frequently used in tractates on kingship (e.g., **57**) to delineate his qualifications and characteristics. It was then only a short step to the use of lists of virtue to specify qualifications for a particular office (e.g., 1 Tim. 3:2–6; 3:8–13; Titus 1:7–9).

57 In this discourse on kingship Dio Chrysostom argues that true kings demonstrate their kingship by their virtue. By way of contrast, he concludes the discourse by taking up the vices of the majority of people. He prefaces his description of the avaricious person by commenting on the characterization of vice and its use in protrepsis. The description itself makes use of lists of vices.

Dio Chrysostom, *Oration* 4.83–96

Now as there are, roughly speaking, three prevailing types of lives which the majority usually adopt, not after thoughtful consideration and testing, I assure you, but because they are carried away by chance and thoughtless impulse, we must affirm that there is just the same number of spirits whom the great mass of foolish humanity follows and serves —some men one spirit and some another—just as a wicked and wanton troop follows a wicked and frenzied leader. Of these types of lives which I have mentioned, the first is luxurious and self-indulgent as regards bodily pleasures, the second, in its turn, is acquisitive and avaricious, while the third is more conspicuous and more disordered than the other two—I mean the one that loves honour and glory—and it manifests a more evident and violent disorder or frenzy, deluding itself into believing that it is enamoured of some noble ideal.

Therefore, come, let us imitate clever artists. They put the impress of their thought and art upon practically everything, representing not only the various gods in human forms but everything else as well. Sometimes they paint rivers in the likeness of men and springs in certain feminine shapes, yes, and islands and cities and well-nigh everything else, like Homer, who boldly represented the Scamander as speaking beneath his flood, and though they cannot give speech to their figures, nevertheless do give them forms and symbols appropriate to their nature, as, for example, their river gods recline, usually naked, and wear long flowing beards and on their heads crowns of tamarisk or rushes. Let us then show ourselves to be no whit worse or less competent in the field of discourse than they in their several arts as we mould and depict the characters of the three spirits of the three lives, therein displaying an accomplishment the reverse of and complementary to the skill and prophetic power of the physiognomists, as they call them. These men can determine and announce a man's character from his shape and appearance; while we propose to draw from a man's habits and acts, a type and shape that will match the physiognomist's work —that is, if we shall succeed in getting hold rather of the average and lower types. Since our purpose is to show the absurdity existing in human lives, there is no impropriety or objection to our being seen imitating poets or artists or, if need be, priests of purification and to our striving to furnish illustrations and examples from every source, in the hope of being able to win souls from evil, delusion, and wicked desires and to lead them to love virtue and to long for a better life; or else we might follow the practice of some of those who deal with initiations and rites of purification, who appease the wrath of Hecate and undertake to make a person sound, and then before the cleansing process, as I understand, set forth and point to the many and various visions that, as they claim, the goddess sends when angry.

Well, then, the avaricious spirit craves gold, silver, lands, cattle, blocks of houses, and every kind of possession. Would it not be represented by a good artist as downcast and gloomy of appearance, humble and mean of dress—aye, as squalid and ragged, loving neither children nor parents nor native land, and recognizing no kinship but that of money, and considering the gods as nothing more than that which reveals to him many vast treasures or the deaths of certain kinsfolk and connections from whom he might inherit, regarding our holy festivals as sheer loss and useless expense, never laughing or smiling, eyeing all with suspicion and thinking them dangerous, distrusting everybody, having a rapacious look, ever twitching his fingers as he computes his own property, I take it, or that of someone else—a spirit not only without appreciation or capacity for any other thing, but scoffing at education and literature except when they have to do with estimates and contracts, the still blinder lover of wealth, which is rightly described and portrayed as blind; mad about every kind of possession and thinking that nothing should be thrown away; unlike the magnetic stone, which they say attracts iron to itself, but amassing copper and lead as well, yes, even sand and rock if anyone gives them, and everywhere and in almost every case regarding possession as more profitable and better than non-possession. He is most frantic and eager, however, to get money, simply because success here is quickest and cheapest, since money goes on piling up day and night and outstrips, I ween, the circuits of the moon. He recks naught of dislike, hate, and curses and, besides, holds that while other kinds of possessions may be pretty baubles wherewith to amuse oneself, money, to put it succinctly, is the very essence of wealth. This, therefore, is what he seeks and pursues from any and every source, never concerning himself at all to ask whether it is acquired by shameful or unjust means, except insofar as, observing the punishments meted out to footpads, he lets cowardice get the better of him and becomes cautious. For he has the soul of a worthless cur, that snatches up things when it expects not to be noticed, and looks on other morsels with longing eyes but keeps away from them, though reluctantly, because the guards are by. So let him be a man insignificant in appearance, servile, unsleeping, never smiling, ever quarrelling and fighting with someone, very much like a pander, who in garb as well as in character is shameless and niggardly, dressed in a coloured mantle, the finery of one of his harlots.

58 This protreptic letter first describes the vicious, then the virtuous condition (cf. Gal. 5:19–23).

Pseudo-Crates, *Epistle* 15

Shun not only the worst of evils, injustice and self-indulgence, but also their causes, pleasures. For you will concentrate on these alone, both present and future, and on nothing else. And pursue not only the best of goods, self-control and perseverance, but also their causes, toils, and do not shun them on account of their harshness. For would you not exchange inferior things for something great? As you would receive gold in exchange for copper, so you would receive virtue in exchange for toils.

LISTS OF HARDSHIPS

Moral philosophers, especially Stoics and Cynics, made extensive use of lists of hardships or unfavorable circumstances in describing themselves or their heroes. Some Stoics classified hardships among those things which are intermediate between virtue and vice (**36a**). While the wise person does not choose them (**31**), philosophy teaches him not to flee from them (**35, 53**). He is to regard them as part of the divine purpose for his life and a means by which he is exercised (**59**). Like an athlete, he engages them in a wrestling match, and conquers them in his struggle to obtain happiness and virtue (**2**). The catalogs of hardships thus paradoxically exhibit his superiority, express his pride, and are a means by which he commends himself (**59, 71**; cf. 1 Cor. 4:9–13; 2 Cor. 4:7–10; 6:3–10; 11:21–29).

59   In this discourse, in which Epictetus describes the ideal philosopher as a Cynic, he constantly has to correct the popular view of Cynics.

Epictetus, *Discourse* 3.22.50–61

Lo, these are words that befit a Cynic, this is his character, and his plan of life. But no, you say, what makes a Cynic is a contemptible wallet, a staff, and big jaws; to devour everything you give him, or to stow it away, or revile tactlessly the people he meets, or to show off his fine shoulder. Do you see the spirit in which you are intending to set your hand to so great an enterprise? First take a mirror, look at your shoulders, find out what kind of loins and thighs you have. Man, it's an Olympic contest in which you are intending to enter your name, not some cheap and miserable contest or other. In the Olympic games it is not possible for you merely to be beaten and then leave; but, in the first place, you needs must disgrace yourself in the sight of the whole civilized world, not merely before the men of Athens, or Lacedaemon, or Nicopolis; and, in the second place, the man who carelessly gets up and leaves must needs be flogged, and before he is flogged he has to suffer thirst, and scorching heat, and swallow quantities of wrestler's sand.

Think the matter over more carefully, know yourself, ask the Deity, do not attempt the task without God. For if God so advises you, be assured that He wishes you either to become great, or to receive many stripes. For this too is a very pleasant strand woven into the Cynic's pattern of life; he must needs be flogged like an ass, and while he is being flogged he must love the men who flog him, as though he were the father or brother of them all. But that is not our way. If someone flogs you, go midst and shout, "O Caesar, what do I have to suffer under your peaceful rule? Let us go before the Proconsul." But what to a Cynic is a Caesar, or a Proconsul, or anyone other than He who has sent him into the world, and whom he serves, that is, Zeus? Does he call upon anyone but Zeus? And is he not persuaded that whatever of these hardships he suffers, Zeus is exercising him? Nay, but Heracles, when he was being exercised by Eurystheus, did not count himself wretched, but used to fulfil without hesitation everything that was enjoined upon him: and yet is this fellow, when he is being trained and exercised by Zeus, prepared to cry out and complain? Is he a man worthy to carry the staff of Diogenes? Hear *his* words to the passers-by as he lies ill of a fever: "Vile wreches," he said, "are you not going to stop? Nay, you are going to take that long, long journey to Olympia, to see the struggle of worthless athletes; but do you not care to see a struggle between a fever and a man?" No doubt a man of *that* sort would have blamed God, who had sent him into the world, for mistreating him! Nay *he* took pride in his distress, and demanded that those who passed should gaze upon him. Why, what will he blame God *for?* Because he is living a decent life? What charge does he bring against Him? The charge that He is exhibiting his virtue in a more brilliant style? Come, what says Diogenes about poverty, death, hardship? How did he habitually compare his happiness with that of the Great King? Or rather, he thought there was no comparison between them. For where there are disturbances, and griefs, and fears, and ineffectual desires, and unsuccessful avoidances, and envies, and jealousies—where is there in the midst of all this a place for happiness to enter? But wherever worthless judgments are held, there all these passions must necessarily exist.

7

Conventional Subjects

The term "topos," which in ancient rhetoric described a topic or intellectual theme by which a speaker or writer made an argument plausible, was also applied to stock treatments of moral subjects. Some scholars think of topoi as clichés—for example, the following on friendship: friendship obtains when souls are drawn together by identical inclinations into an alliance of honorable desires (26, 36d), equality knits friends together (67; cf. Gal. 4:12), friends have all things in common (Acts 4:32), have one soul (Acts 4:32; Phil. 1:27), think the same things (Phil. 2:2), and share in giving and receiving (Phil. 4:15). Others think of a topos as a treatment of a proper thought or action, or of a virtue or a vice, in an independent form larger than a cliché. Still others, recognizing that certain elements occur regularly in the treatment of some subjects, describe topoi as recurring themes. Because of the traditional, standardized way in which the subjects are treated, it is also widely thought that topoi do not deal with existing conditions in the settings envisaged by the literature in which they appear but may anticipate those conditions.

It is more useful, in the study of Greco-Roman morality, to view topoi, as Hierocles (36) does, as traditional, fairly systematic treatments of moral subjects which make use of common clichés, maxims, short definitions, and so forth, without thereby sacrificing an individual viewpoint. Thus a Stoic and an Epicurean could use much of the same traditional material in discussing friendship, but the Stoic would be careful to disavow the utilitarianism he perceived in the Epicurean view of the virtue. The way in which the presuppositions and interests of a writer as well as his desire to distinguish himself from others influenced his use of topoi is reflected in Plutarch's tractate *How to Tell a Flatterer from a Friend* (19, 21), in which he makes use of topoi on friendship, flattery, and frankness. The function to which a topos is put—for example, in protrepsis or

paraenesis or, more narrowly, in consolation—may further determine the way in which it is shaped to apply to the situation at hand.
The following selections represent some of the more common
topoi.

ON THE STATE

Arius Didymus in his handbook takes up many of the subjects also
treated by Hierocles **(36)**. His description of the state is distinguished from Hierocles' **(36b)** by being more academic and descrip-
tive of the constitution.

60

> **Arius Didymus, *Epitome* (Stobaeus 2.7.26=2.150, 1—152, 25
> Wachsmuth). Translated by David L. Balch**
>
> "Concerning politics" these might be the headings. First,
> cities were organized both because man is social by nature
> and because it is useful. Next, the most perfect partnership
> is a city, and a citizen is one who has a claim to civic office.
> A city is the population composed of enough people for a
> self-sufficient life. The population is limited to the degree
> that the city is neither unfeeling nor contemptible, but is
> equipped both to live without want and to take care of those
> who set upon it from the outside. Now household manage-
> ment, lawgiving, politics and making war are various kinds
> of prudence. Household management, as I said, consists in
> financial administration both of a house and of the things
> related to the house. Lawmaking is . . . Politics is . . . Making
> war consists in the theory and financial administration of
> those things useful for the army.
>
> Necessarily, either one, a few or all persons rule cities.
> Each of these is either good or bad. It is good when the
> rulers aim at benefiting the public and bad when they aim at
> their personal interest. The bad is a deviation from the
> good. Monarchy, then, and aristocracy and democracy aim
> at the good, but tyranny, oligarchy and mob-rule aim at the
> bad. The best constitution is some mixture of the good
> forms. But constitutions change many times for the better or
> the worse. In general, the best constitution is the one which
> has been ordered according to virtue, the worst according to
> vice. Ruling, deliberating and judging in democracies is by

all or by a faction or by lot, whereas in oligarchies by resourceful persons and in aristocracies by the best persons.

Seditions in cities occur either rationally or emotionally. They occur rationally whenever those with equal rights are compelled to be unequal, or when those who are unequal have equality. They occur emotionally on account of reputation, love of money, advantage, or ingenuity. Constitutions are destroyed by two causes, either by violence or by fraud. The most stable are those taking care that the public is benefited.

Law courts, senates, assemblies and magistrates are properly defined in constitutions. The most common magistrates are: a priesthood for gods, an army generalship, an admiralty, a superintendence of the market, a controller of the gymnasium, a superintendent of women, a superintendent of children, an office to administer the police and public buildings and streets, a treasury, a guardianship of the laws, an office of tax collection. Some of these are for cities, others for war, and others for harbors and commerce.

The work of a politician is also to reform a constitution, which appears to be much harder than originally to establish one. And the citizenry distribute among themselves the necessary and the earnest occupations. Artisans, menial laborers, farmers, and commercial traders are necessary, for they are underlings to the politicians; but to be fit for every battle and to be able to counsel is more lordly since this involves having charge of virtue and being earnest with respect to the good. Among these the presbyter has chief voice in counsel, and the elder serves the divine, but the young makes war for all. This is the very ancient caste system, first established by Egyptians.

The politician, no less than others, also establishes the rites of the gods in the most prominent places. Private land is to be arranged so that one part is near the frontiers and the other part near the city in order that, since two allotments are distributed to each citizen, both parts of the land might be within easy sight of each other. It is useful to have common meals by law and to pay earnest attention to the public education of the children. For strength and highest perfection of bodies, neither the youngest nor the oldest should marry, for both extremes of age produce deformed children, and the offspring are completely weak. It is to be ordained by law that one is to rear no deformed child, nor to expose a whole child, nor to abort a useful child, I presume. And concerning "politics," these are the main headings.

ON CIVIL CONCORD

Some philosophers assumed civic responsibilities and frequently addressed civic assemblies. Discord, either within a city or between competing cities, was a condition so often encountered that stock arguments and illustrations were developed in speeches advising concord. Dio deliberately uses such traditional illustrations when he refers to cosmic harmony and the cooperation of insects (cf. *1 Clem.* 20). Together with the images of an army (cf. *1 Clem.* 37), a ship, and the human body (63), these were the most popular illustrations used in the topos on unity.

61

Dio Chrysostom, *Oration* 48.14–16

My concern is partly indeed for you, but partly also for myself. For if, when a philosopher has taken a government in hand, he proves unable to produce a united city, this is indeed a shocking state of affairs, one admitting no escape, just as if a shipwright while sailing in a ship should fail to render the ship seaworthy, or as if a man who claimed to be a pilot should swerve toward the wave itself, or as if a builder should obtain a house and, seeing that it was falling to decay, should disregard this fact but, giving it a coat of stucco and a wash of colour, should imagine that he is achieving something.

If my purpose on this occasion were to speak on behalf of concord, I should have had a good deal to say about not only human experiences but celestial also, to the effect that these divine and grand creations, as it happens, require concord and friendship; otherwise there is danger of ruin and destruction for this beautiful work of the creator, the universe. But perhaps I am talking too long, when I should instead go and call the proconsul to our meeting. Accordingly I shall say only this much more—is it not disgraceful that bees are of one mind and no one has ever seen a swarm that is factious and fights against itself, but, on the contrary, they both work and live together, providing food for one another and using it as well? "What!" some one objects, "do we not find there too bees that are called drones, annoying creatures which devour the honey?" Yes, by Heaven, we do indeed; but still the farmers often tolerate even them, not wishing to disturb the hive, and believe it better to waste some of the honey rather than to throw all the bees into confusion. But at Prusa, it may be, there are no lazy drones, buzzing in impotence, sipping the honey. Again, it is a great delight to observe the ants, how contentedly they dwell together, how they go forth from the nest, how they aid one another with their loads, and how they yield the trails to one another. Is it not disgraceful, then, as I was saying, that human beings should be more unintelligent than wild creatures which are so tiny and unintelligent?

ON RETIREMENT

Philosophers sometimes as individuals withdrew from active participation in civic affairs. Some, despairing of bettering people, withdrew and became known as misanthropists (18); others withdrew in protest to some particular policy or official; and others retired to prepare themselves before returning to serve society further. Groups such as the Epicureans withdrew because they thought their ideals could only be realized within their own little communities. Withdrawal could obviously be regarded as criticism, and Seneca reflects a well-placed sensitivity to the opinion of society about such quietism (cf. 1 Thess. 4:9–12; Titus 2:1–10; *Diogn.* 5–6).

62

Seneca, *Epistle* 68.3–6

I now return to the advice which I set out to give you,—that you keep your retirement in the background. There is no need to fasten a placard upon yourself with the words: "Philosopher and Quietist." Give your purpose some other name; call it ill-health and bodily weakness, or merely laziness. To boast of our retirement is but idle self-seeking. Certain animals hide themselves from discovery by confusing the marks of their foot-prints in the neighbourhood of their lairs. You should do the same. Otherwise, there will always be someone dogging your footsteps. Many men pass by that which is visible, and peer after things hidden and concealed; a locked room invites the thief. Things which lie in the open appear cheap; the house-breaker passes by that which is exposed to view. This is the way of the world, and the way of all ignorant men; they crave to burst in upon things. It is therefore best not to vaunt one's retirement. It is, however, a sort of vaunting to make too much of one's concealment and of one's withdrawal from the sight of men. So-and-so has gone into his retreat at Tarentum; that other man has shut himself up at Naples; this third person for many years has not crossed the threshold of his own house. To advertise one's retirement is to collect a crowd. When you withdraw from the world, your business is to talk with yourself, not to have men talk about you.

ON CIVIC RESPONSIBILITY

In this sophistical speech Maximus takes the position that the practical life is better than the contemplative (contrast Luke 10: 38–42). In this popular topos he contrasts the active life to the self-centered, contemplative one and trots out the usual examples of a ship, a city, a building, and the body when arguing for active participation (**36b, 36d, 61**; cf. 1 Cor. 12:14–26; Rom. 12:3–8; Eph. 4:11–16; *1 Clem.* 37.1–38.1).

63

Maximus of Tyre, *Oration* 15.4–5 (*Maximi Tyrii philosophoumena*, ed. H. Hobein [Leipzig: Teubner, 1910], 186–188)

The philosopher has a certain function, but what it is we don't know. "I spend my time in leisure," he says, "by myself I contemplate reality and am filled with truth." You are lucky indeed to have so much leisure! I think that if you boarded a ship you would neither be a pilot, nor a rower, nor one of the sailors who scurry about and contribute to the safety of the ship, nor an agile marine who knows how to handle the ropes or an oar in a calm sea, but rather one of those idle passengers who lie about and are carried around, and for that reason are a burden to the ship. Or do you think that a city has less need of people who would contribute to its safety than a ship at sea? I certainly think there is much greater need on land. For when we are at sea, the number who work is small albeit with a heavy load. But a city is an entity blended together by the cooperation of all. It is the

same way with the body's use, which is of many kinds and
requires many things, and is preserved by the joint contribution of the body's parts to the functioning of the whole: the
feet carry, the eyes see, the ears hear, and so on, lest I waste
time in continuing the list.

If the Phrygian writer of fables wished to compose a fable
in which the foot, out of annoyance with the rest of the body,
and on the ground that it was tired, gave up carrying upright
such a heavy burden and continued to enjoy rest and quiet;
or again, if the molars, on the ground that they were grind
ing and preparing food for so large an idle crowd were
angered and, when asked, refused to pay attention to their
proper work—if these things happened at the same time,
what would result in the fable but the destruction of the
man? That, indeed, is what happens in the political commu-
nion.

ON THE PROFESSIONS

In a society acutely conscious of social position, close attention
was paid to a person's occupation. Despite their differences, Cicero
and Musonius share the conviction that one's professional involve-
ments should not run counter to the values one espouses (cf. James
4:13–14; Hermas, *Vis.* 3.6.5; *Mand.* 3.5; 10.1.4–5; *Sim.* 4.5; 8.8.1–2;
9.20.1–2).

64   Discussions like that of Cicero, with its low estimation of manual labor as servile and base (cf. 1 Cor. 9:19; 2 Cor. 11:7),
represent the views of the advantaged.

Cicero, *On Duties* 1.150–151

In regard to trades and other means of livelihood, which
ones are to be considered becoming to a gentleman and
which ones are vulgar, we have been taught, in general, as
follows. First, those means of livelihood are rejected as un-
desirable which incur people's ill-will, as those of tax-gather-
ers and usurers. Unbecoming to a gentleman, too, and vulgar are the means of livelihood of all hired workmen whom
we pay for mere manual labour, not for artistic skill; for in
their case the very wages they receive is a pledge of their
slavery. Vulgar we must consider those also who buy from
wholesale merchants to retail immediately; for they would
get no profits without a great deal of downright lying; and

verily, there is no action that is meaner than misrepresentation. And all mechanics are engaged in vulgar trades; for no
workshop can have anything liberal about it. Least respect-
able of all are those trades which cater to sensual pleasures:
"Fishmongers, butchers, cooks, and poulterers, and fisher-
men," as Terence says [*The Eunuch* 2.26]. Add to these, if you
please, the perfumers, dancers, and the whole *corps de ballet.*

But the professions in which either a higher degree of
intelligence is required or from which no small benefit to
society is derived—medicine and architecture, for example,
and teaching—these are proper for those whose social position they become. Trade, if it is on a small scale, is to be
considered vulgar; but if wholesale and on a large scale,
importing large quantities from all parts of the world and
distributing to many without misrepresentation, it is not to
be greatly disparaged. Nay, it even seems to deserve the
highest respect, if those who are engaged in it, satiated, or
rather, I should say, satisfied with the fortunes they have
made, make their way from the port to a country estate, as
they have often made it from the sea into port. But of all the
occupations by which gain is secured, none is better than
agriculture, none more profitable, none more delightful,
none more becoming to a freeman.

65   A more favorable attitude toward manual labor, however, is
also found, especially among some Cynics and Stoics (**36f,
53**; cf. Acts 18:3). Whereas Cicero has in mind the managerial
role of a gentleman farmer as a possibly acceptable occupation, Musonius sees value in the philosopher's manual labor on
the land, for it provides him with an opportunity to demonstrate by example what he teaches (cf. 2 Thess. 3:6–10). Thus,
while Musonius earlier in his discussion had considered
how farming might affect his own attempt to live the philosophical life, here he is concerned with how his manual labor
might benefit his students (cf. Acts 20:34–35; 2 Cor. 11:
7–11; Eph. 4:28; 1 Thess. 2:9; contrast *Barn.* 19.10; *Did.*
12.3–4).

Musonius Rufus, *Fragment* **11** *(What Means of Livelihood Is
Appropriate for a Philosopher?)*

What, perhaps someone may say, is it not preposterous for
an educated man who is able to influence the young to the

study of philosophy to work the land and to do manual labor just like a peasant? Yes, that would be really too bad if working the land prevented him from the pursuit of philosophy or from helping others to its attainment. But since that is not so, pupils would seem to me rather benefited by not meeting with their teacher in the city nor listening to his formal lectures and discussions, but by seeing him at work in the fields, demonstrating by his own labor the lessons which philosophy inculcates—that one should endure hardships, and suffer the pains of labor with his own body, rather than depend upon another for sustenance. What is there to prevent a student while he is working from listening to a teacher speaking about self-control or justice or endurance? For those who teach philosophy well do not need many words, nor is there any need that pupils should try to master all this current mass of precepts on which we see our sophists pride themselves; they are enough to consume a whole life-time. But the most necessary and useful things it is not impossible for men to learn in addition to their farm work, especially if they are not kept at work constantly but have periods of rest.

ON SEXUAL CONDUCT

Whatever actual practice may have been, moralists, especially those with Stoic leanings, had conservative views of sex and marriage. Musonius condemns homosexuality, bisexuality, and adultery (**51**). Sexual intercourse is to be confined to marriage (cf. 1 Cor. 7:8–9) and to be engaged in solely for the purpose of procreation (**31, 36g**). While Musonius does have a high view of women, he still reflects traditional attitudes: the woman is the weaker partner (cf. 1 Peter 3:7), and adultery with her wrongs her husband (cf. 1 Thess. 4:6).

66

Musonius Rufus, *Fragment* 12 *(On Sexual Indulgence)*

Not the least significant part of the life of luxury and self-indulgence lies also in sexual excess; for example those who lead such a life crave a variety of loves not only lawful but unlawful ones as well, not women alone but also men; sometimes they pursue one love and sometimes another, and not being satisfied with those which are available, pursue those which are rare and inaccessible, and invent shameful intimacies, all of which constitute a grave indictment of manhood.

Men who are not wantons or immoral are bound to consider sexual intercourse justified only when it occurs in marriage and is indulged in for the purpose of begetting children, since that is lawful, but unjust and unlawful when it is mere pleasure-seeking, even in marriage. But of all sexual relations those involving adultery are most unlawful, and no more tolerable are those of men with men, because it is a monstrous thing and contrary to nature. But, furthermore, leaving out of consideration adultery, all intercourse with women which is without lawful character is shameful and is practiced from lack of self-restraint. So no one with any self-control would think of having relations with a courtesan or a free woman apart from marriage, no, nor even with his own maid-servant. The fact that those relationships are not lawful or seemly makes them a disgrace and a reproach to those seeking them; whence it is that no one dares to do any of these things openly, not even if he has all but lost the ability to blush, and those who are not completely degenerate dare to do these things only in hiding and in secret. And yet to attempt to cover up what one is doing is equivalent to a confession of guilt.

"That's all very well," you say, "but unlike the adulterer who wrongs the husband of the woman he corrupts, the man who has relations with a courtesan or a woman who has no husband wrongs no one for he does not destroy anyone's hope of children." I continue to maintain that everyone who sins and does wrong, even if it affects none of the people about him, yet immediately reveals himself as worse and a less honorable person; for the wrong-doer by the very fact of doing wrong is worse and less honorable. Not to mention the injustice of the thing, there must be sheer wantonness in anyone yielding to the temptation of shameful pleasure and like swine rejoicing in his own vileness. In this category belongs the man who has relations with his own slave-maid, a thing which some people consider quite without shame, since every master is held to have it in his power to use his slave as he wishes. In reply to this I have just one thing to say: if it seems neither shameful nor out of place for a master to have relations with his own slave, particularly if she happens to be unmarried, let him consider how he would like it if his wife had relations with a male slave. Would it not seem completely intolerable not only if the woman who had a lawful husband had relations with a slave, but even if a woman without a husband should have? And yet surely one will not expect men to be less moral than women, nor less capable of disciplining their desires, thereby revealing the stronger in judgment inferior to the weaker, the rulers to the ruled. In fact, it behooves men to be much better if they expect to be superior to women, for surely if they appear to be less self-controlled they will also be baser characters. What need is there to say that it is an act of licentiousness and nothing less for a master to have relations with a slave? Everyone knows that.

ON COVETOUSNESS

Dio's introduction to his discourse on covetousness is an excellent example of a number of characteristics of paraenesis: the self-consciousness with which he repeats what is well known, the function of recollection in the process, the use of medical imagery, the desire to benefit his listeners by making them change, and the quotation from Euripides at the beginning of the topos itself. Covetousness is the greatest social vice (57) and is an attempt to overreach one's brother (cf. 1 Thess. 4:6). It is opposed to equality, which establishes friendship, and deprives people of sufficiency. Already in this initial delineation of the vice, the four topoi of covetousness, equality, friendship, and (self)-sufficiency intersect (cf. 2 Cor. 8: 13–15; 9:5–8; Phil. 4:10–11; 1 Tim. 6:6–10).

67

Dio Chrysostom, *Oration* 17.1–11

The majority of men think that they should speak only on those subjects concerning which the common man has not the true opinion, in order that they may hear and get guidance on the matters whereof they are ignorant; but regarding what is well known and patent to all alike they think it superfluous to instruct. Yet for my own part, if I saw that we were holding to what we believe to be right and were doing nothing out of harmony with the view we already have, I should not myself hold it necessary to insist on matters that are perfectly clear. However, since I observe that it is not our ignorance of the difference between good and evil that hurts us, so much as it is our failure to heed the dictates of reason on these matters and to be true to our personal opinions, I consider it most salutary to remind men of this without ceasing, and to appeal to their reason to give heed and in their acts to observe what is right and proper.

For instance, just as we see physicians and pilots repeating their orders time and again to those under their command, although they were heard the first time—but still they do so when they see them neglectful and unattentive—so too in life it is useful to speak about the same things repeatedly, when the majority know what is their duty, but nevertheless fail to do it. For it is not the main thing that the sick should know what is beneficial to them, but, I suppose, that they should use the treatment; since it is this that will bring them health; nor that men in general should learn what things are helpful and what injurious to their lives, but that they should make no mistake by their choice between these. For just as one may see persons who are suffering from ophthalmia and know that it hurts to put their hands to their eyes, but still are unwilling to refrain from so doing, so likewise in regard to matters in general, the majority, even though they know perfectly well that it is not advantageous to do a certain thing, none the less fall to doing it. Who, for instance, does not know that intemperance is a great evil to its victims? But for all that you can find thousands that are intemperate. Yes, and idleness everybody must certainly know is not only unable to provide the necessaries of life, but, in addition, is destructive of what one already has; and yet in very truth you can find more idlers than men willing to work. Consequently, in my opinion it devolves upon the more thoughtful on all occasions and continually to speak of these matters, in the hope that it may prove possible to make men change their ways and to force them to the better course. For just as in the Mysteries the initiating priest more than once explains beforehand to those who are being initiated each single thing that they must do, in like manner it is profitable that the words concerning things beneficial be repeated often, or rather, all the time, just like some sacred admonition. We know, for instance, that inflamed parts of the body do not yield at once to the first fomentation, but that if the treatment is continued, the swelling is softened and relief is given. So in a like manner we must be well content if we are

able to assuage the inflammation in the souls of the many by
the unceasing use of the word of reason.

So I maintain in regard to covetousness too, that all men
do know it is neither expedient nor honourable, but the
cause of the greatest evils; and that in spite of all this, not
one man refrains from it or is willing to have equality of
possessions with his neighbour. And yet you will find that,
although idleness, intemperance and, to express it in general terms, all the other vices without exception are injurious
to the very men who practice them; and although those who
are addicted to any of them do deservedly, in my opinion,
meet with admonishment and condemnation, still you certainly will find that they are not hated or regarded as the
common enemies of all mankind. But greed is not only the
greatest evil to a man himself, but it injures his neighbours
as well. And so no one pities, forsooth, the covetous man or
cares to instruct him, but all shun him and regard him as
their enemy. If, then, each of those here present wishes to
know the enormity of this wickedness, let him consider how
he himself feels toward those who attempt to overreach him;
for in this way he can get an idea as to how other men must
feel toward him if he is that sort of man. And further, Euripides too, a poet second to none other in reputation, brings
Iocasta on the stage addressing Eteocles and urging him to
refrain from trying to overreach his brother, in some such
words as these [*Phoenician Women* 531–540]:

> At greed, the worst of deities, my son,
> Why graspest thou? Do not; she is Queen of wrong.
> Houses many and happy cities enters she,
> Nor leaves till ruined are her votaries.
> Thou art made for her!—'tis best to venerate
> Equality, which knitteth friends to friends,
> Cities to cities, allies to allies.
> Nature gave men the law of equal rights,
> And the less, ever marshalled against
> The greater, ushers in the dawn of hate.

I have quoted the iambics in full; for when a thought has
been admirably expressed, it marks the man of good sense
to use it in that form.

In this passage, then, are enumerated all the conse-
quences of greed: that it is of advantage neither to the individual nor to the state; but that, on the contrary, it over-

throws and destroys the prosperity of families and states as well; and, in the second place, that the law of men requires us to honour equality, and that this establishes a common bond of friendship and peace for all toward one another, whereas quarrels, internal strife, and foreign wars are due to nothing else than the desire for more, with the result that each side is deprived even of a sufficiency. For what is more necessary than life, or what do all men hold as of more importance than this? But nevertheless men will destroy even that for money, and some too have caused even their own fatherlands to be laid waste. The same poet then goes on to say that there is no greed among the divine beings, wherefore they remain indestructible and ageless, each single one keeping its own proper position night and day and through all the seasons. For, the poet adds, if they were not so ordered, none of them would be able to survive. When, therefore, greed would bring destruction even to the divine beings, what disastrous effect must we believe this malady causes to human kind? And he aptly mentions measures and weights as having been invented to secure justice and to prevent any man from over-reaching another.

ON ANGER

The topic of anger had a firm place in the ancient psychagogical tradition. By Stoics it was classified among those emotions still present in the person making moral progress and consequently was analyzed in their moral psychology (**17**; cf. Hermas, *Mand.* 5.2.4). Plutarch demonstrates the egocentricity with which the subject was often treated: anger is dangerous (cf. *1 Clem.* 39.7; *Did.* 3.2), irrational and unbecoming, thus inimical to the highest human virtues (contrast Rom. 12:17–21; Eph. 4:31–32; James 1:19–20; *1 Clem.* 13). But it appears to be excessive anger that is condemned (Eph. 4:26?); if it is well directed, it can be an ally of virtue. Nevertheless, victory over anger is a qualification for public office (**11**; cf. Titus 1:7; Polycarp, *Phil.* 6.1).

68

Plutarch, *Fragment* 148

All human actions that are done in a rage must be blind and senseless and entirely miss the mark. It is not possible to act

with calculation when acting in a rage, and anything done
without calculation is unskilful and distorted. A man ought,
then, to make reason his guide and so set his hand to life's
task, either pushing aside his feelings of wrath whenever
they assail him, or finding a way past, just as pilots avoid the
waves that bear down upon them. Certainly there is no less
cause for fear, but when a wave of rage comes rolling head
on against a man, he nay capsize and utterly destroy both
himself and his whole family if he does not steer his way
cleverly through it Not that success can be had without
pains and training otherwise men meet with utter disaster.
Those men do best who accept anger as virtue's ally, making
use of it in so far as it is helpful in war and indeed in politics,
but endeavouring to discharge and expel from their souls its
abundance and excess, which we call rage or asperity or
quick temper, disorders that are most unbecoming to manly
hearts. Now what training for this can a grown man practise?
It would seem to me to be the most effective method if we
were to undertake our preliminary practice well in advance
and rid ourselves beforehand of the greatest part of our
temper, for example when dealing with our slaves and in our
relations with our wives. The man who is good-tempered at
home will be much more so in his public life, having been
made in his house and by his household such as to be the
physician of his own soul.

ON SLAVERY AND FREEDOM

The freedom with which the moralists were concerned was the
liberation from vice (**16, 20;** cf. Titus 3:3), especially pleasure (**35**).
Seneca (**17**) defines it as fearing neither man nor the gods, craving
no wickedness or excess, and possessing supreme power over oneself. Freedom is an inner state, hence the paradox that even the
slave may be truly free (**10;** cf. 1 Cor. 7:20–23; Ignatius, *Pol.* 4.3).
Only the good person is free (**69**), but an optimistic view of the
human condition recognizes capacities in people that may allow
them to become free (**10**).

69   Epictetus regards that person as free who recognizes no com-
        pulsion or necessity but exercises freedom of the will (contrast
        1 Cor. 9:15–19; Gal. 5:13).

Epictetus, *Discourse* **4.1.1–5**

> He is free who lives as he wills, who is subject neither to
> compulsion, nor hindrance, nor force, whose choices are
> unhampered, whose desires attain their end, whose aver-
> sions do not fall into what they would avoid. Who, then,
> wishes to live in error?—No one.—Who wishes to live de-
> ceived, impetuous, unjust, unrestrained, peevish, abject?—
> No one.—Therefore, there is no bad man who lives as he
> wills, and accordingly no bad man is free. And who wishes
> to live in grief, fear, envy, pity, desiring things and failing to
> get them, avoiding things and falling into them?—No one at
> all.—Do we find, then, any bad man free from grief or fear,
> not falling into what he would avoid, nor failing to achieve
> what he desires?—No one.—Then we find no bad man free,
> either.

70   Although it is by a philosopher (**10**) or philosophy (**22**) that one
is set free, it is essentially by developing one's reason and
self-discipline that one sets oneself free (**16;** contrast Rom.
6:15–23; Gal. 5:1).

Pseudo-Crates, *Epistle* **7**

> [Addressed to the wealthy.] Go hang yourselves, for al-
> though you have lupines, dried figs, water, and Megarian
> tunics, you engage in trade and cultivate much land, you are
> guilty of treachery, you exercise tyranny and commit mur-
> der, and you perpetrate whatever other such things there are
> —despite the fact that one should live quietly. But as for us,
> we observe complete peace since we have been freed from
> every evil by Diogenes of Sinope, and although we possess
> nothing, we have everything, but you, though you have ev-
> erything, really have nothing because of your rivalry, jeal-
> ousy, fear, and conceit.

ON THE ARMOR OF THE SAGE

As the Stoics used athletic imagery (**2, 59**) to describe their struggle with and victory over the passions, so they used military metaphors to describe the sage's security. The wise man depends on
nobody but himself. Trusting in his own wisdom, prudence, and

self-control, he shows that he is superior to the world **(11)**. Full of human and divine virtues, safe in the high citadel of his reason, he is protected by high, impregnable walls which no siege can breach (cf. 2 Cor. 10:3–6. See also Rom. 13:12–14; Eph. 6:11–17; 1 Thess. 5:8; Polycarp, *Phil.* 4.1, all of which have Jewish roots).

71

Seneca, *On the Firmness of the Wise Man* 6.3–8

But here is one who comes into our midst and says: "There is no reason why you should doubt that a mortal man can raise himself above his human lot, that he can view with unconcern pains and losses, sores and wounds, and nature's great commotions as she rages all around him, can bear hardship calmly and prosperity soberly, neither yielding to the one nor trusting to the other; that he can remain wholly unchanged amid the diversities of fortune and count nothing but himself his own, and of this self, even, only its better part. See, here am I to prove to you this—that, though beneath the hand of that destroyer of so many cities fortifications shaken by the battering-ram may totter, and high towers undermined by tunnels and secret saps may sink in sudden downfall, and earthworks rise to match the loftiest citadel, yet no war-engines can be devised that will shake the firm-fixed soul. I crept just now from the ruins of my house, and while the conflagration blazed on every side, I fled from the flames through blood; what fate befalls my daughters, whether a worse one than their country's own, I know not. Alone and old, and seeing the enemy in possession of everything around me, I, nevertheless, declare that my holdings are all intact and unharmed. I still possess them; whatever I have had as my own, I have. There is no reason for you to suppose me vanquished and yourself the victor; your fortune has vanquished my fortune. Where those things are that pass and change their owners, I know not; so far as my possessions are concerned, they are with me, and ever will be with me. The losers are yonder rich men who have lost their estates—the libertines who have lost their loves—the prostitutes whom they cherished at a great expenditure of shame —politicians who have lost the senate-house, the forum, and the places appointed for the public exercise of their failings; the usurers have lost their records on which their avarice, rejoicing without warrant, based its dream on wealth. But I have still my all, untouched and undiminished. Do you, accordingly, put your question to those who weep and wail, who, in defence of their money, present their naked bodies to the point of the sword, who, when their pockets are loaded, flee from the enemy." Know, therefore, Serenus, that this perfect man, full of virtues human and divine, can lose nothing. His goods are girt about by strong and insurmountable defences. Not Babylon's walls, which an Alexander entered, are to be compared with these, not the ramparts of Carthage or Numantia, both captured by one man's hand, not the Capitol or citadel of Rome,—upon them the enemy has left his marks. The walls which guard the wise man are safe from both flame and assault, they provide no means of entrance,—are lofty, impregnable, godlike.

Bibliography

Introduction

Bultmann, Rudolf. *Theology of the New Testament.* 2 vols. Translated by Kendrick Grobel. New York: Charles Scribner's Sons, 1951.

Dihle, Albrecht. "Ethik." In *Reallexikon für Antike und Christentum* 6 (1966): 646–796.

Enslin, Morton Scott. *The Ethics of Paul.* Reprint. Nashville: Abingdon Press, 1962.

Meeks, Wayne A. *The Moral World of the First Christians.* Philadelphia: Westminster Press, 1986.

Schrage, Wolfgang. *Ethik des Neuen Testaments.* Grundrisse zum Neuen Testament. NTD Ergänzungsreihe 4. Göttingen: Vandenhoeck und Ruprecht, 1982.

Chapter 1: The Social Settings of Moral Instruction

Dill, Samuel. *Roman Society from Nero to Marcus Aurelius.* New York: Macmillan, 1905.

Stowers, Stanley Kent. "Social Status, Public Speaking and Private Teaching: The Circumstances of Paul's Preaching Activity," *Novum Testamentum* 26 (1984): 59–82.

Chapter 2: Aims and Character of the Moral Teacher

Friedländer, Ludwig. *Roman Life and Manners Under the Early Empire,* Vol. 3. Translated by L. A. Magnus. New York: E. P. Dutton, 1913.

Nock, Arthur Darby. *Conversion: The Old and the New in Religion from Alexander to Augustine of Hippo.* Oxford: Clarendon Press, 1933.

Wendland, Paul. *Die hellenistisch-römische Kultur in ihren Beziehungen zu Judentum und Christentum.* HNT 1, 3. Tübingen: J. C. B. Mohr, 1912.

Chapter 3: Methods of Instruction and Moral Nurture

Hadot, Ilsetraut. *Seneca und die griechisch-römische Tradition der Seelenleitung.* Berlin: Walter de Gruyter, 1969.

Malherbe, Abraham J. " 'Gentle as a Nurse': The Cynic Background to I Thess ii." *Novum Testamentum* 12 (1970): 203–217.

———. " 'In Season and Out of Season': 2 Timothy 4:2." *Journal of Biblical Literature* 103 (1984): 235–243.

Rabbow, Paul. *Seelenführung: Methodik der Exerzitien in der Antike.* Munich: Kösel-Verlag, 1954.

Chapter 4: Means of Instruction

Balch, David L. *Let Wives Be Submissive: The Domestic Code in 1 Peter.* SBL Monograph Series, 26. Chico, Calif.: Scholars Press, 1981.

Berger, K. "Hellenistische Gattungen im Neuen Testament." In *Aufstieg und Niedergang der römischen Welt*, Part 2, Vol. 25. 2, edited by Wolfgang Haase. Berlin: Walter de Gruyter, 1984. 1031–1432, 1831–1885.

Bonner, Stanley F. *Education in Ancient Rome.* Berkeley and Los Angeles: University of California Press, 1977.

Chadwick, Henry. "Florilegium." *Reallexikon für Antike und Christentum*, 7 (1969): 1131–1160.

Dibelius, Martin. *A Fresh Approach to the New Testament and Early Christian Literature.* New York: Charles Scribner's Sons, 1936.

Chapter 5: Styles of Exhortation

Malherbe, Abraham J. "Hellenistic Moralists and the New Testament." In *Aufstieg und Niedergang der römischen Welt*, Part 2, Vol. 27, edited by Wolfgang Haase and Hildegard Temporini. Berlin: Walter de Gruyter. Forthcoming.

Stowers, Stanley Kent. *The Diatribe and Paul's Letter to the Romans.* SBL Dissertation Series, 57. Chico, Calif.: Scholars Press, 1981.

Chapter 6: Literary and Rhetorical Conventions

Vögtle, Anton. *Die Tugend- und Lasterkataloge im Neuen Testament: Exegetisch, religions- und formgeschichtlich untersucht.* Neutestamentliche Abhandlungen 16, 4/5. Münster: Aschendorff, 1936.

Chapter 7: Conventional Subjects

Betz, Hans Dieter. *Plutarch's Ethical Writings and Early Christian Literature.* Studia ad Corpus Hellenisticum, 4. Leiden: E. J. Brill, 1978.

Ferguson, John. *Moral Values in the Ancient World.* London: Methuen, 1958.

Theological Dictionary of the New Testament. Edited by Gerhard Kittel and Gerhard Friedrich; translated by Geoffrey W. Bromiley. 10 vols. Grand Rapids: Wm. B. Eerdmans Publishing Co., 1964–1976.

Index of Names

Academy, 54
Achilles, 54, 124
Aeschylus, 115
Aesop, 73
Aetolia, 52
Agamemnon, 54
Aglaonice, 109
Alexander, 24, 79, 161
Amasis, 72
Ammonius, 49
Antigenidas, 138
Antisthenes, 18, 26
Apollo, 21, 73, 77, 78
Aristippus, 112, 114
Aristophanes, 78
Aristotle, 65, 71, 122
Arius Didymus, 17, 145
Arrian, 18, 23
Artaxerxes, 79
Asclepius, 77
Athens, 18, 19, 39, 114, 123, 142
Attica, 77

Babylon, 77, 161
Bias, 72
Bion of Borysthenes, 129
Bithynia, 20
Brontinus, 21

Caesar, 143
Calvus, 127
Carthage, 161
Cato, 67
Celsus, 11
Chaeronea, 21

Chios, 77
Chiron, 77
Chronos, 115
Cicero, 13, 17, 79, 150, 151
Cleanthes, 65, 67, 119, 124
Clement of Alexandria, 121, 122
Corinth, 18, 26–27, 39, 112
Craneion, 26
Crates, 17, 35, 79, 141, 159
Curetes, 59

Demetrius the Cynic, 21
Demetrius of Phalerum, 18, 80, 82
Demonax, 136
Dio Chrysostom, 18, 20, 24, 26, 37, 42, 50, 116, 129, 147, 154
Diogenes, 17, 18, 26–28, 35, 38, 42, 47, 54, 73–79, 112, 114, 139, 143, 159
Diogenes Laertius, 18, 19, 33, 105, 112
Dion, 79
Dionysius, 79, 112, 114, 115
Domitian, 18

Ennodius, 121
Epictetus, 13, 18, 20, 24, 36, 67, 122, 129, 130, 142, 158, 159
Epicurus, 18, 19, 33, 62, 63, 79, 105, 120
Epimenides, 115
Eteocles, 156
Eubule, 83
Eupolis, 58

Euripides, 50, 52, 53, 60, 115, 116, 154, 156
Eurydice, 107, 108
Eurystheus, 143

Ferentinum, 113

Gorgias, 107–108

Hecate, 140
Hecato, 65
Hector, 53, 54
Hegetor, 109
Heracles, 52, 53, 135, 136, 143
Hermarchus, 63, 65
Hesiod, 74
Hierocles, 19, 30, 85–104, 144, 145
Hipparchia, 17
Hipponicus, 126
Homer, 39, 40, 50, 51, 53, 54, 57, 59, 77, 87, 95, 102, 109, 115, 133, 139
Horace, 19, 113

Ismenias, 137
Isocrates, 19, 122, 125

Julian, 19, 35, 39
Justin Martyr, 121

Kleareta, 83

Lacedaemon, 142
Laelius, 67
Lesbos, 77
Lucian, 20, 34, 39, 57, 136
Lucilius, 21, 62, 64, 69
Lucius, 20
Lycon, 78
Lycurgus, 77, 79

Maximus of Tyre, 20, 24, 71–73, 129, 149
Melanthius, 107
Melissa, 20, 79, 83
Melitus, 78
Menander, 115
Metrocles, 112
Metrodorus, 62, 65, 112

Miletus, 113
Minucius Felix, 122
Musonius Rufus, 13, 18, 20, 24, 31–33, 41, 42, 129, 132, 150, 151, 152

Nero, 21
Nestor, 54
Nicopolis, 142
Nigrinus, 57
Numantia, 161

Odysseus, 54
Olympia, 107
Oxyrhynchus, 20, 82

Phidias, 91
Phrygia, 59
Plato, 48, 55, 65, 67, 78, 87, 108, 109, 112, 123
Pliny the Elder, 20
Pliny the Younger, 20, 55
Plutarch, 12, 21, 23, 48, 50, 53, 60, 71, 93, 107, 115, 117, 129, 137, 144, 157
Polemo, 55–57
Pollianus, 107, 108
Polyaenus, 65
Poseidon, 26
Prodicus, 135
Prometheus, 73
Prusa, 18
Ptolemy, 122
Pythagoras, 21, 48, 110, 117, 118

Rhea, 59
Rome, 19, 161

Sardanapalus, 84
Saturn, 74, 77
Scaeva, 113
Scamander, 139
Scythia, 59
Seneca, 14, 21, 24, 41, 43, 62, 64, 65, 66, 68, 69, 79, 117, 118, 120, 127, 129, 138, 148, 158, 160
Serapio, 69
Sextus Empiricus, 21, 33
Sicily, 79, 114, 115
Socrates, 49, 65, 67, 78, 79, 94, 114, 123, 124, 133, 135

Solon, 77, 78, 79
Sophocles, 54, 115, 116
Sostratus, 136
Sparta, 51
Stilbo, 120
Stobaeus, 19, 20, 85
Syracuse, 79, 112

Telephus, 60
Teles, 129
Terence, 151
Theano, 21, 79, 83
Theodorus, 112, 113
Theon, 109

Theophrastus, 71
Timoxena, 108
Trajan, 20

Vatinius, 127
Virgil, 115

Xenocrates, 55, 72
Xenophon, 79, 109, 135

Zaleucus, 90
Zeno, 65, 67, 119, 124
Zeus, 32, 39, 73, 74, 77, 78, 88, 89,
    91, 92, 94, 100, 102, 143

Index of Subjects

abortion, 147

abuse, 52; characteristic of philosophers, 40; technique in soul care, 51

accusation(s): against philosophers, 39–40; by philosophers, 40; to elicit repentance, 49

adaptation: of frankness, 55; of traditions to circumstances, 50–51, 65–66

admonition, 52, 73, 80, 81, 92, 94, 155, 156; in letters, 80, 81; in private, 49–50, 51; in public, 50, 51; response to, 60; technique in soul care, 48, 49, 55; see also censure; correction; frankness; rebuke; reproach; reproof

adornment, 83

adultery, 29, 128, 153–154

adversity: see hardship

advice, 28, 127

affliction: see hardship

aid, moral, 51

aim, of moral philosophers, 30, 73, 121

alarm, technique in soul care, 54

allegories of Pythagoras, 118

ambition, 45, 61

ancients, 66; helpers in moral progress, 63

anecdote: see chreiai

anger, 45, 50, 157–158; ally of virtue, 157; victory over, 37–38, 157–158

antithesis, 24, 25, 73, 76–77, 125, 136, 138

apophthegm, 112

applause: not courted by philosophy, 64

arrogance, 39, 134

arts, 41, 42, 139

asceticism, 37

association: with base persons, 117; with hedonists, 112; with parents, 92–93; with philosophers, 134

athletic imagery, 26, 27, 72, 126, 142, 159

avarice: see greed

beneficence, 91, 94; divine, 87

benefit, 65, 72, 95, 146, 155; of frank speech, 35; of philosophy, 30–31, 60

body, 102; as metaphor, 88, 89, 93, 95, 150; training, 52; see also athletic imagery

boldness, 115; see also frankness

brother, 82, 97; part of oneself, 95; treatment of, 93–95

carping, 40, 51; see also abuse

censure, 113, 125; characteristic of Cynics, 35; letter of, 81; of philosophers in general, 40; see also admonition

change, of the self, 64, 73, 76, 155, 94; societal, rejected, 90

children, 50, 52, 77, 82, 89, 94, 111, 114; education of, 13, 23, 30–31,

115, 117–118, 146; exposure of, 99, 103, 147; fruit of marriage, 101; helpers, 99, 101, 103; rearing of, 83–85; their conduct toward parents, 90–93; *see also* procreation

choice, for philosophical life, 55, 75–77, 78

chreiai, 111–115, 117; in compilations, 119; different from gnomes, 109

Christians: attitudes toward pagan morality, 14–15, 30; letters of, 80; literature of, 13–14, 15, 23, 68, 85, 109–110, 122

citizenship, 88–90, 145

comfort: *see* consolation

commendation, prior to frank speech, 53

common topic: *see* topos

community: laws and customs, 90; philosophic, 13

compilations, 14, 25, 105–120; for memorization, 119; poetry, 115; popularity of, 119; use in schools, 115, 117; for wives, 108

compulsion, 32, 147, 158

concord: civic, 81, 261–263, 266; household, 188; *see also* harmony

condemnation of vice-ridden, 156

conflict, inner, 124

consolation, 48, 125, 127, 128, 145; letters of, 80, 82

constitution, 88, 90, 104, 145–147; *see also* state

contention, 51

contentiousness, 37, 49, 54

contest, hardships as, 27

conversion, 56–59, 73, 76, 122, 124

cooperation, 266; *see also* harmony

correction, 60, 92; *see also* admonition

corruption, 47, 52

counsel: need for, 127; regarding relatives, 97

courage, 133

courtesan, 25, 153

covetousness, 154–157; *see also* greed

cowardice, 54

crowds, 26

customs, 33; superiority of ancient, 88, 90

Cynic(s), 12, 13, 14, 18, 20, 24–25, 26, 28, 39, 40, 41, 46, 50, 73, 82, 112, 113, 136, 142, 151; ideal, 35–36, 142–143

death, fear of, 46, 75, 106, 133

decorum, 83

deeds: ancient models, 62; importance of, *see* word and deed

defenses of the wise person, 38

depravity, 52; *see also* human condition

desire(s), 46, 51, 52, 92, 106, 143; *see also* greed; covetousness

dialogical style, 362

diatribe, 18, 20, 36, 129–134; definition, 129; typical features, 129–130; usage, 129

disease of the soul, 43–46, 47, 49, 52–53, 75, 90, 138

disquiet, 34, 61

divine scheme, 36

dogmatists, 21, 33

drunkenness, as metaphor, 58

duties, 128, 155; to fatherland, 88–90; to gods, 86–88; of husband and wife, 97–99; in lists, 30–31; of mother, 83–85; to parents, 90–93

earnestness, 61

eclecticism, 12, 21

education, 13, 23, 30–31, 105, 109, 115–116, 117–118, 132–134, 146; *see also* schools; learning; students

effeminacy, 60, 98

Egyptians, 146

eloquence, 68

encouragement, 63; *see also* help

endurance, 113, 152

envy, 32, 37, 51, 143

Epicureans, 12, 13, 14, 19, 33, 39, 48, 144, 148

epideixis, 121, 122

epitome, 23, 85–104, 118

equality, 146, 156, 157

error, correction of, 48, 50, 53–55

evil, 34, 46, 47, 76, 85–86, 106, 123, 127, 128, 140; causes of, 86, 87–88, 156

example, 39, 62, 63, 65, 73, 125, 127, 134, 135–136, 137, 139, 140; ancient, 63; of bad persons, 137–138; father as, 125–126, 136, 137; philosopher as, 36, 64, 152; of vice, 140–141; of virtue (Diogenes), 77; *see also* help; imitation
exhortation, 33, 48, 51, 52, 81, 92, 127, 129; in consolation, 81; effectiveness of, 94; purpose, 124; styles, 121–134
extravagance, 88, 108

fame, 105
family, 57, 82, 93, 96–97, 104; *see also* brother; children; father; *Haustafel;* husband; parents; wife
father(s), 32, 50, 52, 53, 97; as model, 125–126, 136, 137
fatherland, 88–90, 157; *see also* state
fear, 38, 46, 64, 76, 106, 143
firmness, of sage, 38, 159–161
flattery, 35, 47, 60, 72, 83
folly, 51
fool(s), 62
foolishness, 52, 60
fortune, 35, 95, 106
forum, 24
frankness, 25, 35, 48–50, 53–55, 61, 121; *see also* admonition
freedom, 36–37, 42, 46, 51, 57, 67, 73, 75, 76, 77, 78, 159; and slavery, 158–159; and volition, 159
friend(s) and friendship, 31, 49, 52, 53, 54, 64, 65, 69, 77, 89, 93, 95, 103, 104, 110, 118, 127, 144, 154, 157

gentleness, 50, 51, 55, 60, 111
gnomes, 109–111
god(s), 11, 15, 31, 36, 46, 73–74, 75, 89, 102, 103, 110, 111, 140; call of philosopher by, 142–143; as causes of good, 87; conduct toward, 86–88, 126; fatherland as, 89; as inflicting punishment, 87; laws as, 90; parents as, 91–92; sage as messenger of, 36; will of, 25, 32; Zeus, 32, 39, 73, 143; *see also* providence

gold: ridiculed by philosopher, 57; women to avoid, 83
Golden Age, 72–74
Golden Race, 74
Golden Rule, 93–94, 126
good, the, 36, 41–42, 45, 46, 65, 84, 86, 87, 105, 122, 123, 127, 128, 145
goodwill, 53, 54, 97, 101, 104
gratitude, 91, 130
greed, 31, 45, 51, 88, 133, 140–141, 156–157, 160; *see also* covetousness
grief, 50, 52, 143
guidance: *see* help
guide: *see* example

handbooks, 17, 19, 80, 85, 117
happiness, 13, 15, 27, 33, 36, 44, 76, 120, 124, 142, 143
hardship(s), 26, 27, 73, 84, 120, 152, 160; as contest, 142; as divine exercise, 143; and divine purpose, 142; as exhibition of virtue, 143; lists of, 84, 88, 141–143; pride in, 143
harmony: civic 51, 147–148, 149; cosmic, 147–148; within household, 108; with nature, 67, 100
harshness, 51
Haustafel, 19, 85–86, 127, 132; definition, 135; *see also* duties
hearing, 28, 59, 71–72, 124
hedonism, 12, 112
help: in achieving moral salvation, 48–49, 62–64, 108; children as, 99, 101, 103; wives as, 101–102; *see also* example
helplessness, 42
homosexuality, 15, 152, 153
honor: love of, 139; rejected by philosopher, 35, 52, 57
hope, 64
hospitality, 116
household, 24, 88, 95, 100, 108, 135, 158; management of, 83, 97–99, 132, 134, 145; *see also Haustafel*
human condition, 40–47, 62–64, 74–75, 122, 158
husband, 50, 83; duties of, 97–99

ideal person, 28, 76–78
idleness, 118, 155, 156
ignorance, 42, 52, 54, 62, 64, 103, 111, 123, 155; and error, 92
imitation, 100, 125, 126, 135, 137, 138, 139; *see also* example
imprudence, 102
inclination to virtue, 59; *see also* human condition
independence, 52, 77; *see also* freedom
individuals, instruction of, 48, 50
individuality, 51
injustice, 88, 141, 153
innovation, as suspect, 88, 90
insects, as models, 147–148
insolence, 52
intemperance, 51, 55–56, 134, 155, 156
intermediate things, 87–88
introspection, 35
ironic wishes, 130

jealousy, 51, 52, 54, 143
Judaism, 11
justice, 86, 118, 126, 128, 133, 152

kindness, 52
kings and kingship, 31, 37, 77,
Koine, philosophical, 12

labor, manual, 52, 98, 133, 146, 150, 151–152; *see also* occupations
laws, 103; as gods, 90
learning, 59–62, 65, 66, 119; *see also* education
lecture hall, 23, 24, 65, 85, 123
leisure, 149
letters, 43, 68, 79–85
licentiousness, 54, 154
living voice, 65, 71, 120; *see also* speech
love, 93–95, 97
lover(s), 50, 58, 128
lust, 38, 45, 51, 88
luxury, 84, 98, 116, 152

malice, 32
marriage, 78, 90, 99–104, 107, 128, 146; advantages of, 101–102; advice on, 107–109; as natural, 100; for procreation, 102–103; sexual relations in, 153; *see also* husband; procreation; wife
matter, 88
maxims, 19, 21, 109, 115, 119, 120, 126, 144
meanness, 63
medical imagery, 25, 26, 30, 34, 41, 43, 44, 47, 49, 52, 53, 55, 60, 64, 66, 70, 88, 123, 134, 155
memorization, 105, 115, 119, 127
memory, 69, 225
messenger, sage as, 36
military imagery, 38, 51, 59, 104, 119, 159–161
misanthropy, 12
misconduct, 61
model: *see* example
moderation, 31; in frankness, 55
modesty, 39, 50, 60, 71, 83, 126, 134
money, 34, 42, 109, 140, 146, 157
moral purpose, 67
mother, 52, 83–85, 97
motives: for preaching, 24; of true philosophers, 34

nature, 13, 34, 41, 60, 80, 84, 95, 103, 106, 120, 125; harmony with, 67, 100; life according to, 88, 92, 131; and marriage, 99–100, 103; things against, 88, 153
nurses, 73

occupations, 98–99, 146, 150–152; *see also* duties; labor
old age, 33, 53; children as help in, 103; respect for, 108; weakness of, 92

pain, 38, 55, 84
paradigm: *see* example
paradox, 130
paraenesis, 80, 82, 93, 124–129, 136, 138, 145, 154; adaptation, 65–67, 124–128; definition, 124–125; relation to protrepsis, 121, 124–125; types, 129

parents, 89, 90–93, 94, 95, 97, 103; conduct toward, 90–93, 126; as gods, 91–92; *see also* father; mother
passion, 37–38, 45–46, 143, 159, 284; *see also* anger; disease; lust
perfection, 45
Peripatetics, 12, 14
persuasion, 50–51
philosopher(s), 11–13, 24–25, 32, 37–38, 39, 41, 68, 109, 117, 121, 123, 149; criticism of, 39–40; and government, 147; ideal, 25, 36, 77–78, 142–143; manner of life, 38; means of livelihood, 151–152; self-defense by, 34; speech of, 68–71
philosophy, 12, 13, 32, 57, 58, 61, 64, 70, 85, 108, 115–116, 122, 127, 128; benefits, 24; goal, 30–34, 121; Koine, 12; and moral life, 11–12; practical nature, 30–31, 127, 134; study of, 32–33, 117, by women, 109, 132–134
Phrygians, 97
physician: *see* medical imagery
pity, 51
Platonists, 12, 15
pleasure(s), 31, 32, 34, 37–38, 40, 42, 46, 51, 56, 72, 75, 76, 83–84, 105–106, 108, 110, 139, 141, 153, 158
poetry, 25, 86–87; in moral instruction, 115–117
politics: *see* state
poverty, 39, 75, 103, 114, 116, 117, 143
praise, 94, 122, 123, 129
precepts, 69, 93, 107, 127, 128, 138
predecessors, 66
procreation, 101–104, 153; pleasing to parents, 103; societal duty, 104; when inadvisable, 146
professions: *see* occupations
progress, 28, 38, 43, 45, 61–65, 67, 119, 126, 157
prostitute, 25, 153
protrepsis, 33, 55, 57, 71, 72, 122–124, 129, 136, 138, 141, 144; relation to paraenesis, 121, 124–125

proverb, 119
providence, 26, 36, 73, 111, 130–132
prudence, 38, 128, 145, 159
psychagogy, 48
punishment, 82; divine, 11, 86–87
Pythagorean(s), 12, 14, 15, 20, 21, 82–85

reading, 65
reason, 32, 35, 51, 77, 81, 100, 107, 132, 134, 155, 158
rebuke, 49, 81, 84, 92; *see also* admonition
reception of speech, 123
reciprocity, 90, 93
recollection, 58, 154; *see also* reminder
reconciliation, 36
religion and ethics, 11–12
reminder, 49, 51, 114, 125, 127, 128, 155
repentance, 49, 51, 56, 86
repetition of exhortations, 155
reproach, 40, 51; *see also* admonition
reproof, 24, 36, 39, 60–61, 78; exposes human condition, 122; *see also* admonition
reputation, 34, 42, 57, 146
response to instruction, 55–59
responsibility, 60, 149–150
retaliation, 93
retirement, 106, 148–150
reverence for predecessors, 66
reviling, 26, 48, 142; *see also* abuse; carping; scolding
rhetoric, 68
riches: *see* wealth
righteousness, 51
rivalry, 61

sage: *see* wise person
salvation, 60, 62
sample: *see* example; imitation
schools, 13, 23, 109, 115, 117, 129; *see also* education
scolding, 129; *see also* reviling
scout, sage as, 36
security, 105, 106; of sage, 159–160; provided by children, 104

self-control, 31, 37–38, 88, 98, 126, 133, 134, 141, 152, 153, 154, 158, 160
self-evaluation, 35, 142
self-indulgence, 139, 141, 152
self-interest, 64
self-love, 93, 94
self-sufficiency, 13, 40, 112–114, 120, 145, 154, 157
serenity, 36, 118; *see also* tranquillity
settings for instruction, 13, 15, 23, 24–25, 41, 48
sexual conduct, 29, 128, 152–154
sexual intercourse, 131, 153
shame, 31, 56, 60, 61–62, 108
shamelessness, 51
silence, 110
simplicity, 38
Skeptic(s), 12, 14, 17, 21, 33, 39
slave(s), 31, 37, 56, 78, 133, 134, 153, 158; of emotion, 84; of pleasure, 78, 84; treatment of, 94
slavery, 36, 37, 51, 56, 158–159
sobriety, 31, 51, 56, 58
social relations, 93; *see also* harmony; *Haustafel*
soft living, 51
sorrow, 54
soul(s), 59, 95; as business of philosophy, 44; care, 92; *see also* disease
Spartans, 137
speech, 71, 118; ambrosial, 57; empty, 70; preferred means of instruction, 68; proper style of, 68–71, 122–124; *see also* living voice; rhetoric; word
state, 104, 145–147, 156; conduct toward, 88–90; opposition to, 13; well-being of, 88; *see also* constitution; fatherland; politics
steadfastness, 51
stinginess, 54
Stoics, 12, 13, 14, 15, 18, 20, 21, 30, 36, 39, 43, 73, 82, 85–86, 99, 119, 120, 141–142, 144, 151–152, 157, 159
strife, 51
students, 50; disciples, 40; *see also* education
stupidity, 52

style: of letters, 80–8?· of the philosopher, 69
suffering, 34, 55; causes of, 88; *see also* hardship(s)
sympathy, 54

teaching, 23, 28, 50, 53, 57, 65, 108, 119; reverence due teacher, 66; *see also* education
temper, 54
temperance, 40, 56, 58, 83
therapy, of the word, 71
threat, in letters, 80, 81
toil, 63, 125, 141; *see also* labor
topos, 85–86, 94, 103, 135; definition and use of, 144–145, 147, 154–155
tradition, 50–51, 65–66, 69
tranquillity, 33, 46; *see also* serenity
transformation by philosophy, 55–57, 64–65; *see also* conversion
Two Ways (image), 135

unity, 147; *see also* harmony
utterances, 60

vice, 13, 34, 43, 45, 46, 49, 71, 87–88, 95, 135, 145, 154, 156; examples, 139–141; lists, 37, 39, 42, 45–46, 159; usage of lists, 73, 130, 136, 138
virtue, 13, 15, 40, 41–42, 43, 46, 51, 56, 61, 62, 66, 72, 75, 83, 84, 86, 88, 118, 126, 135, 140, 141, 142, 143, 145, 157, 160; cardinal, 20, 132; compared to vice, 74; exhibition of, 143; gift from God, 86; inclination to, 59, 132; lists, 32; usage of lists, 73, 130, 136, 138
volition, 25, 55, 56, 62, 73, 78, 81, 86, 87, 95, 104

warning, 129
weakness, 51, 60, 103, 123
wealth, 39, 40, 52, 57, 74, 77, 103, 106, 110, 116, 117, 120, 125, 140; 161; *see also* gold; money
wife, 50, 83, 89, 108, 114, 158; advantages afforded by, 101–102;

wife (*cont.*)
duties of, 97–99, 101, 132; not burdensome, 102; respect for, 108; sexual conduct of, 153
will: *see* volition
wisdom, 38, 44, 45, 63, 65, 118; as art, 28; search for, 33; as treasure, 66
wise person, 26, 35, 77–78, 106, 159–161; and marriage, 99; security, 161; superiority, 34, 37–38, 138, 142, 160; uniqueness, 110;

see also philosopher
women, 82–83; dress of, 83; duties of, 132–133; education of, 109, 132–134; morality of, 108, 154; self-control of, 133; *see also* marriage; mother; wife
word, 69; cleaves the soul, 59; and deed, 38–39, 43–44, 51, 64, 65, 73, 78, 110; as sage's ally, 38; spoken, 65, 80; *see also* living voice; recollection
workshop, 24

Index of New Testament References

Matthew
chs. 5–7 85
5:29. 110
5:39. 110
5:39–42 93
7:12. 93
7:13–14 135
15:1–9 88
15:5–6 90
15:19 138
16:4. 110
18:15 48
19:3–6 100
19:18–19 105
23:2–7 135
23:3. 38

Mark
12:13–17 88

Luke
6:5 111
6:20–49 85
6:31. 93
8:13. 60
10:38–42 149
12:13–14 111
17:20–21 111
21:1–4 112

Acts
2:37–42 57
4:32. 144
5:39. 115
13:14ff. 23
14:8ff. 23
17:1ff. 23
17:11 60
17:16ff. 23

17:22–30 42
17:28 116
18:3. 151
18:4ff. 23
18:7ff. 23
19:8–10 23
20:31 . . . . . 48, 50
20:31–34 125
20:31–35 130
20:34–35 151
26:14 115
26:25 23

Romans
1:1 36
1:18–31 42
1:29–31 130
1:31. 138
2:1 38
2:1, 3 130
2:4 86
2:21–23 . . . . 38, 130
3:1–8 130
4:1 129
4:23. 65
6:1 129
6:15–23 159
6:16. 130
7:15–20 62
9:19. 129
9:19–24 130
9:20. 130
ch. 12 125
12:2. . . . . . . 33, 64
12:3–8 149
12:3–21 93
12:6–8 130
12:17–21 157
12:21 93

ch. 13 125
13:1–7 88
13:12–14 160
14:7. 130
15:4. 65
15:14 48
15:18 38
16:1–2 80
16:22 68

1 Corinthians
1:1 36
2:1–5 68
3:1–3 60
3:5–9 130
3:16. 130
3:18. 35
4:7, 8 130
4:9–13 142
4:14–17 . . 57, 125, 136
4:14–21 80
4:17. 35
5:1 14
5:6 130
5:11. 96
6:1–6 96
6:1–8 93
6:2 130
6:9–10 130
6:9–11 . . . . . 14, 138
6:15. 130
7:8–9 . . . . . 99, 152
7:10–11 65
7:17. 65
7:20–23 158
7:28. 99
7:29–31 130
7:32–35 100
ch. 9 136

1 Corinthians *(cont.)*

9:1 130
9:4–6 130
9:9f. 65
9:15–19 158
9:19 150
9:19–22 130
9:19–23 50
9:24 130
9:24–27 26
10:1–13 136
10:6 86
10:10–11 65
10:11 86
10:13 86
10:32 14
12:12–26 93
12:14–26 149
12:29–30 130
14:24–25 57
15:8–10 37
15:33 . . . . . 115, 130
15:35 . . . . . 129, 130
15:36 130

2 Corinthians

4:7–10 142
4:8–9 130
6:3–10 142
6:9–10 130
7:10 86
8:13–15 154
9:1 125
9:5–8 154
10:1 47
10:3–6 160
10:10 . . . . . . 68, 79
10:11 39
11:1 130
11:7 150
11:7–11 151
11:21–29 138
12:14 90

Galatians

1:11–17 37
1:15 36
4:12 144
5:1 159
5:12 130
5:13 158
5:19–23 . . . 138, 141
5:21 138
5:23 138
6:1 48
6:1–5 28
6:10 93

Ephesians

2:1–3 14
4:11–16 149
4:26 157
4:28 151
4:31–32 157
5:3–4 71
5:15–17 33
5:22–6:9 85
6:1–4 90
6:4 23
6:11–17 160

Philippians

1:27 144
2:2 144
2:25–30 57
3:4–11 36
3:4–13 34
3:14 26
4:8–9 136
4:10–11 154
4:15 144
4:21–23 80

Colossians

3:1–17 64
3:5–17 138
3:7 138
3:12–13 138
3:18–4:1 85
3:20–21 90
4:5 14
4:6 71

1 Thessalonians . . 80
chs. 1–3 136
1:4 96
1:5, 6 125
2:1–8 . . . 23, 125, 136
2:2 125
2:5 125
2:7 . . . . 46, 50
2:9 . . . . . . 125, 151
2:11 . . . . 48, 50, 125
2:13 60
3:4 125
3:6 125
3:6–10 57
3:10 60
4:1 125
4:3 32
4:3–8 10
4:5 14
4:6 . . . . . . 152, 154
4:9 125
4:9–12 148

4:10 125
4:12 14
4:13–18 82
4:18 82
5:1 125
5:8 160
5:11 . . . . . . 48, 125
5:12–15 48
5:27 68

2 Thessalonians

2:13 96
3:6–10 151
3:6–13 135
3:7–9 125
3:14–15 28
3:15 93

1 Timothy

1:8–10 138
1:9–10 138
1:10 138
1:12–17 37
2:1–7 98
2:9 82
2:15 99
3:1–2 88
3:2–6 139
3:4–5 . . . . . . 82, 107
3:5 100
3:7 14
3:8–13 139
3:11–12 82
3:12 100
3:12–13 107
4:11–12 135
4:11–16 . . . . . . : 35
4:13 48
4:13–16 71
4:15 43
5:1 48
5:3–16 82
5:4 90
5:8 90
5:9–16 97
5:10 82
5:14 . . . . . . 99, 100
6:1 14
6:2 48
6:3–5 . . . . . . 43, 138
6:6–10 154
6:10 109

2 Timothy 136
1:5 . . . . . . 23, 136
2:1–9 136
2:5 26

2:10–15 136
2:16–17 43
2:24–25 71
2:24–26 50
3:2 93
3:2–5 138
3:8 136
3:15 23
4:2 . . . . 48, 53
4:7–8 26

Titus
1:7 157
1:7–9 139
1:9 122
1:12 115
1:13 122
1:15 43
2:1–10 . . . . 82, 85,
148
2:4–5 82
2:5 14
2:8 14
2:10 14
2:11 31
2:12 31
2:15 122
3:1 88
3:1–7 138
3:3 . . . . . . 14, 158
3:7–8 35
3:8–10 28

Philemon 80
15–16 96

Hebrews 68
3:13 48
5:11–14 60
10:25 48
10:32–33 26
11:4–38 135
12:1 26
12:5–11 86
13:1–19 124
13:7 135
13:8 86

James 124, 129
ch. 1 125
1:1 80
1:12 26
1:13–14 86
1:18 129
1:19–20 157
1:21 60
1:22–25 60
ch. 2 125
2:14–16 130
2:18 129
2:18–26 136
2:20–21 130
2:20–23 62
ch. 3 125
3:1–12 69
3:13 39
3:13–18 138
4:13–14 150

1 Peter
1:13–19 42

1:18 14
1:18–19 88
1:22–2:10 64
2:1–2 138
2:11–5:11 124
2:12 14
2:13–17 88
2:13–3:12 85
2:15 . . . . 14, 33
2:21–25 136
2:23 93
3:1 14
3:1–6 . . . . . 82, 107
3:3–4 82
3:5–6 . . . . . . 62, 136
3:7 152
3:8–9 93
3:16 14

2 Peter
1:3–7 86
1:5–7 138
2:4–8 136
3:9 86

1 John 68
3:18 38

3 John 80

Jude
6–7 136

Revelation
1:3 68

Index of Apostolic Fathers References

Barnabas
chs. 18–20 . . 124, 135
19.4. 48
19.8. 82
19.10 151

1 Clement. 80, 136
1.1 14
1.3 . . . . . . 82, 85, 97
3.5 138
chs. 4–5 136
chs. 4–39. 124
7.1 34
chs. 9–12. 135
ch. 13 . . . . 138, 157
chs. 17–18 135
ch. 20 . . . . 135, 147
21.6–9 85
21.7. 82
21.8. 82
30.3. 38
ch. 37 147
37.1–38.1 149
39.7. 157
47.7. 14
ch. 55 135
56.2. 48
60.4–61.2 88

2 Clement. 68
ch. 4 39
17.2. 48
ch. 19 57

Didache
chs. 1–6 135
3.2 157
4.9 82
12.3–4 151

Diognetus. 122
chs. 5–6 148

Hermas, *Mandates* . . .
68, 125
chs. 2–5 138
3.3 57
3.5 150
5.1.1 138
5.2.4 157
8.10. 138
10.1.4–5 150
12.4. 57

Hermas, *Similitudes*
4.5 150
8.8.1–2 150
9.20.1–2 150

Hermas, *Visions*
1.1.5 122
3.6.5 150
3.9.10 48

Ignatius, *Ephesians*
4.1 125
15.1. 38

Ignatius, *Polycarp*
1.2 . . . . 48, 125
1.3 50
chs. 4–5 85
4.2 50
4.3 158

Ignatius, *Trallians*
2.2 125
8.2 14

Polycarp, *Philippians*
4.1 . . . . 34, 160
4.2 82
chs. 4–5 85
6.1 157
chs. 8–9 135
12.3. 88